DEVON
BUILDING

For W.G. Hoskins

DEVON BUILDING

An introduction to local
traditions

Edited by Peter Beacham

DEVON BOOKS

First published in Great Britain in 1990 by Devon Books
Second edition 1995
Third edition 2001

British Library Cataloguing-in-Publication Data
A CIP record for this title is available from the British Library

ISBN 1 85522 808 4

Published with the support of the Devon County Council Environment Directorate and English Heritage

DEVON BOOKS
OFFICIAL PUBLISHER TO DEVON COUNTY COUNCIL

Halsgrove House
Lower Moor Way
Tiverton, Devon EX16 6SS
Tel: 01884 243242
Fax: 01884 243325
email sales@halsgrove.com
website www.halsgrove.com

Printed and bound in Great Britain by Hackman Print Ltd, Rhondda

Contents

Acknowledgements

Among students of local history in England, those of his native county have particular cause to acknowledge the debt they owe to W.G. Hoskins. So it is a special pleasure that he has accepted the dedication of this book, marking his personal interest in its subject and his particular service to Devon County Council as Historic Buildings Consultant from 1968–1978.

One of the great delights of working in Devon is the ready co-operation which has characterized this field of study and which finds expression in this book. It is a collaborative effort not just in the obvious sense that it is a collection of essays by four different contributors but because the individual essays reflect the work of other colleagues over many years. Devon was especially fortunate that Nat Alcock took such interest in the county in the 1960s when the study of local building history began to flourish. His prodigious early research (see Bibliography) not only figured large in the emerging picture of vernacular building studies in Britain and abroad but gave an important stimulus to further research in Devon. There are many like the present editor who owe their earliest introduction to Devon buildings to him. Apart from the present writers, other early workers included Charles Hulland, Elizabeth Gawne and Kay Coutin, whose valuable contributions, like those of other members of the Vernacular Architecture Group, are interwoven into the essays in this book.

Another substantial contribution has been made by the Exeter Museums Archaeological Field Unit. Under the direction of Chris Henderson, the unit has undertaken building recording and research not only in Exeter but all over Devon to the great benefit of the county. The unit has supplied much information, some of it unpublished, for this book as well as some of the illustrations.

The study of Devon's rural building history has been greatly advanced in recent years by the Department of the Environment's official revision of the statutory lists of buildings of special architectural and historic interest. The survey work was undertaken on behalf of English Heritage by Architecton of Bristol, and particular acknowledgement is due to Martin Robertson and Peter Chapman of English Heritage, John Schofield and Colin Harvey of Architecton, and Martin Cherry, Jenny Chesher, Jo Cox, Michael Laithwaite, James Moir and John Thorp the field workers.

More particular acknowledgement from the contributors is due to the following people and organizations: from Peter Child to Roger Robinson for his help with the farm buildings of the South Hams and to Richard Coates for an introduction to the buildings and archives of the Rolle (Clinton Devon) Estate; from Michael Laithwaite to John Allan, the late W.P. Authers, Trevor Miles, Captain H.G. Pertwee CBE DSO RN, Henrietta Quinnell and John Thorp; from John Thorp to Michael Laithwaite and the MSC Barnstaple Historic Building re-survey team (1985–86) and to the RIBA for a research grant. The invaluable help of the many photographic and illustrative contributors is acknowledged elsewhere, but the book owes much to Brian Blakeway for his specially commissioned reconstruction drawings and to James Ravilious for his superlative photographs which so help the visual imagination in picturing the human (and animal) life which sheltered in these buildings. I also wish to acknowledge the help I have received from Kate Procter of the Dartmoor National Park Authority for the plans of Higher Uppacott and Lower Jurston.

It is a pleasure to acknowledge the help of colleagues in the Property Department of Devon County Council under its Director, Andrew Smy. It was the initiative of Peter Hunt, the Amenities and Countryside Officer, that inspired this publication. The Amenities and Countryside Committee made a generous grant towards publication costs. Judith Heywood, Karen Farrell, Lyne Fielding and their colleagues in the Support

Services Division patiently and skilfully translated the many and varied manuscripts into typescripts.

The necessarily detailed systematic investigations on which these essays are based would have been impossible without the co-operation and hospitality of countless individuals who own or occupy these buildings. Often to their inconvenience we have been allowed to crawl into the most inaccessible parts of their houses, sometimes several times with a seemingly never ending succession of colleagues. Such sympathetic owners are as good a safeguard for our historic buildings as any historic buildings legislation. We owe it to all of them to emphasize that the inclusion of a building in this book does not imply that it is open to the public, a point of particular importance because these are almost all modest buildings which are homes, not museums.

Finally, two more personal editorial acknowledgements. I should like to record my appreciation of the help I have always received from my fellow contributors for I have learned much from them over the many years of our collaboration. And I owe my family a special tribute because they have patiently endured my preoccupation with this publication over many more supposedly free evenings and weekends than I ever intended.

Peter Beacham 1990

Preface to the 2001 edition

Ten years on from the original publication of this book, it is good to be able to report that further subsequent research has both confirmed the broad picture we sketched out then, and considerably enhanced the detail. The significance of Devon's building traditions in the national and international context has been heightened as dendrochronological dating has shown the county's medieval buildings to be even older than we dared suggest, while Devon's smoke-blackened thatch is now recognised as an outstanding archaeobotanical resource in the wider European context. We have therefore added a new chapter by Jo Cox and John Thorp who have undertaken much relevant research on both these topics, and on local slating traditions.

There is a larger reason for welcoming the chance to publish a new edition, and that concerns the contribution that local building traditions make to the unique character of Devon. As development pressure increases inexorably in these crowded islands year on year, the importance of local distinctiveness, cultural diversity and regional identity has at last begun to achieve political recognition. Devon County Council has been a pioneer in promoting such environmentally sensitive thinking, and now English Heritage, in reviewing policy on the historic environment for Government on behalf of the heritage sector, has made characterization – the understanding of the uniqueness of place – the cornerstone of our recommendations for future national policy.

Understanding *Power of Place*, as our report to Government is aptly titled, ought to be the starting point for the regeneration of rural and urban Britain's built environment. A profound understanding of history should inspire our future development, and *Devon Building* has much that is relevant to say about such issues. As rural Devon begins to recover from the devastating effects of foot and mouth disease, it is clear that change is likely to be even more radical than in the last decade of the twentieth century. We need to heed the messages of this book more urgently than ever in the early years of this new millennium.

Peter Beacham
London, August 2001

Farm near Lapford. The traditional close interweaving of farmhouse and farmyard activities is increasingly rare.

Introduction

PETER BEACHAM

We live in a period of intense activity and interest in the local building history of England. There are more eager purchasers for our smaller historic houses than there are such properties to buy. Once acquired, such houses are often lavished with more restoration and improvement than is good for their historic integrity. Buildings which have become redundant for their original function are enthusiastically sought out and converted into new homes. A plethora of books and manuals is suddenly available to guide (or confuse) the owner, visitor or student. And local and national conservation groups flourish as the conservation of historic buildings has become a significant component of the planning and development process.

Compared with just twenty years ago, there has been a rapid change in attitudes towards what is sometimes called the historic built environment. But it is not all gain, even in the relatively favoured world of building conservation.[1] Behind the heady movements of the property market are radical social and economic changes in the patterns of life which have fashioned the English landscape and townscape. Such changes have very considerable implications for the fate of our stock of historic buildings. In urban areas, for example, the replacement of a multitude of small local shops by large scale commercial development is now affecting small historic towns as well as major city centres; it is in such small towns that a wealth of early town houses survives. The countryside is already living through an increasingly unquiet revolution as the farm buildings of the traditional farmstead are declared redundant for modern agriculture and revamped into houses.

Those of us who have to present the arguments for the conservation of our local buildings, whether individually to the new owner of a small historic house or publicly to a planning inquiry into a city centre redevelopment, know how vulnerable these relatively modest buildings are. In typically Devonian fashion, many of them disguise their true historic riches from the outside world. Their significance and distinctiveness needs constant restatement; the vast majority of the 25000 or so statutorily protected buildings in Devon are individually of vital local significance rather than of national importance. Such buildings are invaluable because they represent the cultural, social and economic history of a particular locality. Collectively, it is these buildings rather than the nationally recognized monuments that help to distinguish one place from another and thus characterize this county as Devon rather than any other part of England.

Official recognition of the significance of our local traditional buildings is based upon the listing of buildings of special

Cob barn for sale at Dowland. Planning permission for conversion to residential use means the destruction or radical alteration of former farm buildings.

buildings are cared for by their owners and how applications to alter them are handled by local planning authorities and English Heritage. The precarious future of the longhouse is a good example of this issue; even though the Devon longhouse has received national recognition (most of the surviving examples now enjoy Grade II* status), applications are still being received to destroy the original shippon ends of the few survivors by conversion to domestic use. This illustrates the truth that, whatever the strictures of historic building law, however vigorous and vigilant local government, and however well informed are conservation groups, architects and builders, there is no substitute for the understanding and thoughtful owner.

It is therefore the primary purpose of this book to stimulate interest in and further understanding of the distinctive building history of Devon. The local building traditions of the county flourished in the centuries between 1400 and about 1800, before they were gradually diluted by more general national influences and materials; and it is upon this period that these essays are sharply focused. Any such chronological definition has its drawbacks. In the case of farm buildings, the nineteenth century was of particular importance so the period is extended forward to allow discussion of nineteenth-century developments on the farmstead. Other building types such as church and priests' houses[2] and mills that belong to the period of the fourteenth to eighteenth centuries are not included in the present volume; perhaps this book will stimulate research and publication of these building types. The modest later eighteenth- and nineteenth-century houses that contribute so much to the distinctive character of the streets of the small market towns and larger villages are also not included. They too should be celebrated in a future publication, for such buildings are becoming increasingly easy prey to insensitive development.

In the book I have outlined a general picture of 'local building materials and methods'. Research into the oral history of this subject would yield particularly rich results since many local traditions are still very much alive in the memories of retired craftsmen and builders. Peter Child's essay on 'farmhouse building traditions' was first published over a decade ago.[3] Although he has revised it in the light of subsequent research, and especially the re-survey of rural Devon already mentioned, the substance remains unaltered, a tribute to its original accuracy. I have written separately on 'the longhouse' because of

architectural and historic interest. It is heartening that the recent government sponsored re-survey of most of rural Devon has much improved the official protection of the smaller fifteenth- to eighteenth-century houses of the countryside and added greatly to our knowledge about their distribution. The comprehensive descriptions of the houses in the new published lists are models of their kind and should prove of immense value in the future care of the buildings. Inevitably, this very considerable achievement has also served to reveal the inadequacy of the older lists covering most of Devon's historic towns where many older houses are threatened by relatively large scale re-developments. And even the new rural lists do not seriously tackle the issue of farm buildings deserving official protection, largely because we lack well researched criteria for selection. So we shall still need to be vigilant to ensure that our locally important buildings are properly protected by the listing process.

Listing alone is not, of course, enough. It simply marks out a bulding as being of historic interest. What matters is how such

Bridgetown, Iddesleigh. A typical Devon farmstead comprising an older house (in this case sixteenth and seventeenth century) surrounded by later and more modest farm buildings.

Burrington. Such unpretentious houses line the streets of most Devon villages and market towns, often disguising earlier building phases behind relatively late fronts.

Devon's nationally important concentration of this house type. Peter Child has contributed a pioneering study of 'farm buildings' which should provide a firm basis for further research. This is urgently needed because of the speed with which farm buildings are being converted into residential hamlets. It would be particularly valuable to record the buildings of the farm and, again because it is still accessible, the oral history of how the farmstead worked.

Michael Laithwaite first published his original essay on 'town houses up to 1660' in the 1970s.[4] Here again his general thesis has been substaned and amplified by the considerable subsequent research which has been occasioned by the significant number of urban developments. The essay has consequently been thoroughly revised to include references to important new discoveries and it now presents a summary of nearly a quarter of a century's personal research. Revision has also enabled a more logical division of the seventeenth century to be adopted allowing John Thorp to write on 'late seventeenth- and early eighteenth-century town houses'. This important essay also reflects the author's extensive research on urban building in the county and focuses on two nationally significant concentrations of buildings of this period at Bideford and Topsham.

The final section of the book, again by John Thorp and also breaking new ground, is about 'wall painting and lime plaster decoration', a Devon speciality of national importance. The subject matter of this essay is, by its nature, particularly vulnerable to accidental destruction, so it is perhaps appropriate to end with some characteristically common-sense advice from W.G. Hoskins. 'At least let us know what we are doing when we do what seems a rather harmless thing. We may be destroying something that need not be destroyed.'[5] And that of course goes for much more than plasterwork.

1

Local Building Materials and Methods

PETER BEACHAM

It is already difficult in the late twentieth century to appreciate how different modern building is from the traditional technology evolved over many centuries which it has replaced so suddenly and so recently. This difficulty is often all too apparent when inappropriate materials and methods are applied to older buildings which have depended for their technical performance over as much as 500 years on a radically different technology. Fortunately the links in the chain of tradition are now starting to be rediscovered and reassembled in an upsurge of interest in the skills, crafts, and materials which were used to construct our local buildings. We need to understand them if we are to understand how our older buildings work; only then can we apply such knowledge, in combination with appropriate modern technology, to their continuing care and repair.

The different forms of smaller buildings found in Devon from between about 1400 until sometime after 1800 are regional variations of building patterns discernible during this period throughout Great Britain and even further afield (for example Brittany can be usefully compared with South West England).[1] They look and feel distinctly Devonian because they are interpretations of these national patterns into a local idiom. Visually this is most obvious by their use of Devon building materials and methods but it is also achieved by subtle adaptations of standard types, plan forms and even decorative details to suit local conditions and ambitions. As a result no one building of this period is exactly the same as another.

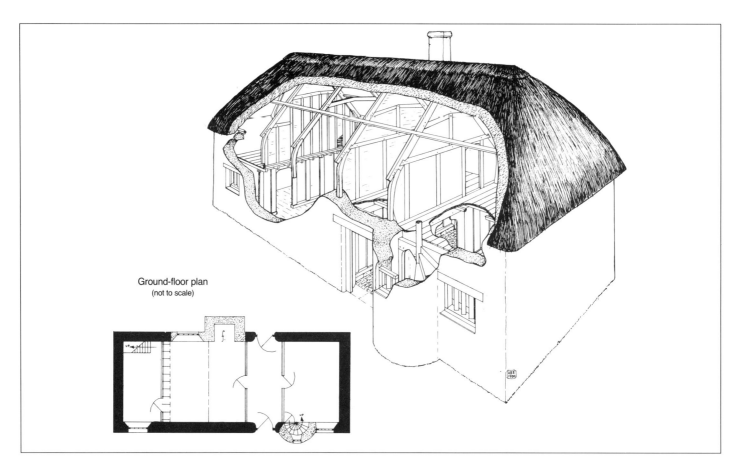

Ground-floor plan
(not to scale)

Timber

Although in a vast and diverse rural county like Devon it would be foolish to draw too rigid a distinction between town and country, detailed examination of large numbers of historic structures throughout the county indicates some fundamental differences. In building construction this is seen in the use of timber framing as a walling technique. In the countryside there is an unchallenged tradition of solid external walls, the only exceptions being some timber-framed porches of the seventeenth century (e.g. Spencer's Cottage, Colebrooke), a few very rare

1.1. *A three-room cross-passage house typical of rural Devon. The external walls are of solid construction (here cob) but all the internal partitions are timber framed. The house is shown in a late sixteenth-century phase when, although much partitioning has occurred and a chimney stack added to the lateral rear wall, the hall is still open to the roof.*

examples of sections of partly timber-framed walls in east Devon, e.g. much of the added east wing of Pale House, Kerswell, and at Langford Court, Plymtree, Poltimore Farm, Farway, and some eighteenth-century granaries. Internally it is a different story, for timber-framed internal partitions, either original or inserted, are very common in rural houses (1.1). Indeed a vigorous carpentry tradition which includes accomplished roof carpentry and other high-quality features like stud and panel screens and moulded

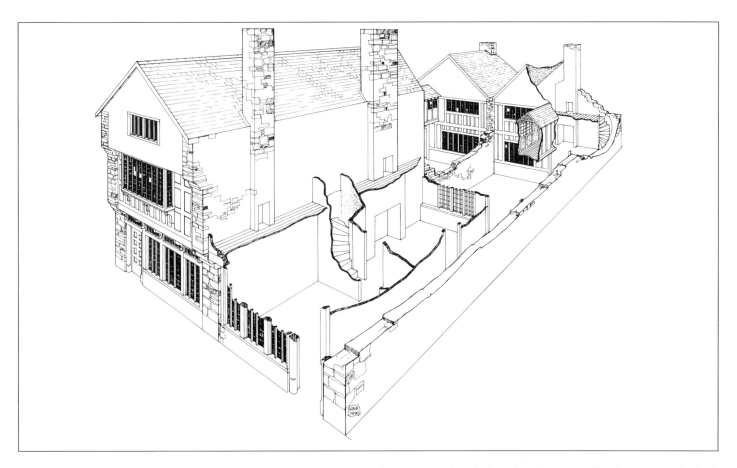

1.2. A Devon town house of c. 1650, based on Totnes examples. Such houses are built on long narrow building plots which produce this characteristic plan form of a front and back block here linked by a first floor gallery. Between the solid stone side walls with neighbouring properties which incorporate chimneys for both houses, timber framing is used for the front and back walls of the buildings.

and framed ceilings is one of the outstanding features of the rural house; they are described in more detail in the account of farmhouse building traditions.

In contrast, although rural construction techniques (and house types) do occur in Devon towns, timber-framed external walls are very common in town houses of the sixteenth to eighteenth centuries, which are sometimes three- and four-storey buildings in contrast to the rural house of one or two storeys only. Timber

framing is found in what is generally known as 'mixed construction': here the houses have solid side walls but completely timber-framed front and often back walls. The framing shows some development over the period. In the few surviving medieval town houses it consists of widely spaced vertical studs with large downward braces halved across the uprights with little embellishment. Later framing is built around small rectangular moulded panels usually combined with oriel windows. This framing was intended to be exposed and it is even exuberantly decorated in the seventeenth-century houses of Exeter, Dartmouth, Plymouth, Topsham and Totnes where it is also jettied out at successive storey levels on the street elevation. But exposed timber framing went out of fashion by 1660, so

1.3. Devon cruck construction. True (Pilleven, Witheridge), jointed (Bury Barton, Lapford) and upper (Pizwell, Postbridge) crucks

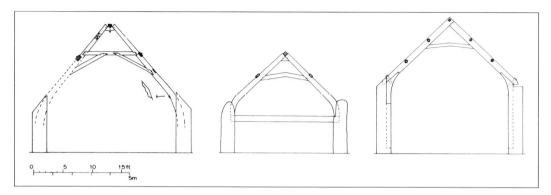

1.4. Cruck variations: (left) Ayshford, Burlescombe: cruck wall post extending to ground level (right) Lower Allerton, Dartington: short cruck

much earlier framing was later covered by slate cladding or plaster or the house was completely re-fronted. More modest later houses are always rendered or slate clad as is the case with the seventeenth- to nineteenth-century houses of Ashburton. Examples are described in detail under the accounts of town houses in Chapters 5 and 6.

Timber was also used extensively for windows, door frames and doors which were often decoratively moulded. This is not easy to appreciate today because so many houses have lost such features through decay and replacement. There are some rare survivals of houses with a more or less complete display of seventeenth-century window carpentry (e.g. Woodbeer Court, Plymtree; Middlecombe, Hockworthy; and Great Gutton, Shobrooke), but it is more common to find the odd ovolo-moulded survival among nineteenth-century casements. There are even rare medieval survivors like the hall window of Little Hackworthy, Tedburn St Mary.

The difference between rural and urban wall construction in timber is reinforced by distinctions in roof construction of the fifteenth to seventeenth centuries. Rural Devon is one of the most important areas in Great Britain for cruck construction.[2] This is a technique whereby a roof truss is formed of two timbers rising from each side of the building at ground level, curving through eaves level and carrying to the ridge where they meet (1.3). Such a technique is more appropriate for a building with timber framed external walls because the cruck and not the walls carry the thrust of the roof. But in rural Devon these ubiquitous crucks of the fifteenth to seventeenth centuries are set not into timber framing but into solid walls of cob and stone (1.4). And, equally curiously, crucks are rare in towns, though they are not unknown (e.g. 38 High Street, Barnstaple).

Bearing this in mind, it is particularly difficult to explain the most distinctive form of Devon cruck, the jointed cruck. What is certain is that such crucks are *not* reused ship's timbers as is often popularly supposed because of their curved shape. It is possible that the cruck form was deliberately employed to achieve something of the effect of the gothic arch in the open hall. In this jointed cruck construction, each cruck is of two timbers, a wall post and a principal rafter, jointed at eaves level by a mortice and tenon joint with side pegs or faced pegged with a slip tenon (usually considered an early technique). Other variations include the scarf joint and the side lapped joint. The length of the wall

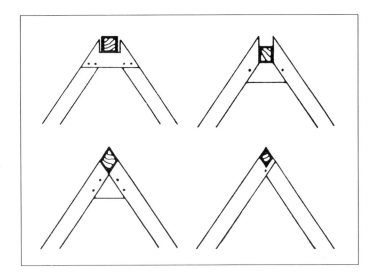

1.5. *Roof apexes of the fifteenth to seventeenth centuries*

post varies considerably from examples that reach the ground (there are massive examples at Ayshford, Burlescombe) to vestigially short legs at the other extreme, particularly in the South Hams. Some trusses have a variant form in which the principal rafter has a slightly curved foot where it enters the wall; another variation has straight principals jointed onto short legs set in the top of the wall, an apparently seventeenth-century form.

There are also examples of true crucks in Devon though they are much rarer than the jointed form. Chimsworthy, Bratton Clovelly and Pilleven, Witheridge, both have massive true cruck trusses mixed with jointed crucks. Also common is the end or hip cruck, a curved timber carrying from the middle of the end wall to the ridge. Raised crucks also make rare appearances in Devon.

Though many fifteenth- to eighteenth-century roofs are of straightforward carpentry, rural Devon does show some elaboration in the earlier phases. Particularly over the hall section of the open hall roof, the central truss can be arch-braced and the collar cambered, sometimes with wind bracing and even chamfered edges to all the roof members (plate 2). Roof apexes can be structurally complex earlier in the period and show some evolution from linked to jointed construction (1.5). Another

1.6. Cob in building construction. (Top) Boycombe, Farway: cob used as the infill (daub) of a wattle panel
(Bottom) Hennard, Germansweek: cob chimney

apparently decorative feature is the way in which the pegs in the carpentry joints can be left fully expressed even in a roof of superior quality such as Rudge, Morchard Bishop. But elaborate decoration such as that found at South Yard, Rose Ash, is not a Devonian tradition. Where more elaborate medieval roofs occur in these local buildings they are generally an indication that a house has come down the social scale, usually from a small manor house to a farm house. Examples are the false hammer beam roof at Traymill, Thorverton; the devolved crown post roofs at Parsonage Farm, Newton Ferrers, Clifford Barton, Dunsford and the Old Rectory, Cheriton Bishop; the base cruck roofs at Moorestone, Halberton, Bridford Barton, Bridford (one of the earliest roofs in Devon) and Uplowman Court, Uplowman; and the common rafter roofs with arch braces at Fishley Barton, Tawstock and Woodbeer Court, Plymtree.

Cob

Cob is simply the Devon word for the mud wall and no other county in England has as much mud walling as Devon. This is usually offered as evidence for both the primitive nature of the technique and material, and also the backwardness of building construction in the West Country. Neither contention squares with the facts. Although this mass walling technique has unbroken continuity in the history of house construction all over the world, it must not be seen as a primitive building method restricted to peasant housing. It is the traditional means of mass wall construction throughout much of rural Devon during the period of the fourteenth to ninteenth centuries, though it is found less commonly in towns especially those more prosperous in the past. It is used for the whole constructional range from the simple garden wall or pig sty to the most substantial yeoman's house. In some houses it is employed for building the chimney stack as well as the wall (the Ley Arms, Kenn; Spanishlake Cottage, Doddiscombsleigh) and it is also found infilling internal timber-framed partitions mostly as wattle and daub or occasionally as cob bricks (Acorn Cottage, Thorverton). Even in grander buildings like Church House, South Tawton or Shilstone, Throwleigh; it is used to heighten medieval walls, sometimes to allow the insertion of first floor windows when an open-hall

1.7. *Farmyard at Bridgetown, Iddesleigh. Cob uses on-site sub soil, and was often mixed by cattle treading.*

1.8. Cob construction at Alfred Howard's yard, Morchard Road, Down St Mary. The sequence shows (top left) sub-soil and straw being mixed (bottom left) cob ready for building (right) lifting and laying a new 'raise'.

house was converted to a two-storied building, but often to facilitate the bedding-in of the roof carpentry (1.6).

As for the conservatism of the cob building tradition in Devon, J.R. Harrison has argued that there are good technical reasons for the superiority of cob over against both the national preference for the timber frame or a direct evolutionary move to stone walling. In 'The Mud Wall in England',[3] the only national study of the nature of materials used in mud wall construction, Harrison concludes that it is the excellence of the material, derived from the Culm measures and the Devonian slates and shales, that made Devon 'the heartland of the technique in the west'. This is primarily due to the low level of volumetric instability (susceptibility to shrinkage and expansion) in these clay sub soils and the availability of a first rate aggregate (the flat slatey fragments known as 'shillet'), as well as the special skills of Devon cob builders.

The basic material for cob walling is always on-site sub soil but there is immense variety in Devon cob walls. This is a result of the widely differing nature of the sub soils in a geologically complex county and local variations in the techniques of mixing and building. 'Red' cob from the red Devon sandstones could be prepared relatively simply by adding straw but the resultant unrendered wall is not highly weather resistant as the sand easily washes out. Elsewhere the mixing process could be more complex involving the introduction of aggregates as well as straw into the clay; this mixture was sometimes allowed to weather over winter before construction began, but the finished product, even unrendered, is immensely strong and hardwearing. Straw was added primarily to overcome shrinkage problems, which it did by spreading hairline fractures along each fibre throughout the wall mass. To a lesser extent it facilitated mixing and hanging the wet cob on the pitch fork while raising onto the wall. Dung was sometimes added as a 'plasticiser' for similar reasons.

Both mixing and raising cob is extremely heavy and labour intensive work (1.8); sometimes the mixing was therefore achieved by cattle treading. The wet cob was then raised up onto the wall in small amounts by a pitch fork. There it was trodden and tamped down until firm, roughly pared off, and left to set. It would be pared back to the building line when it had achieved its initial set, after which it would continue to harden over a much longer period. The next layer could not be raised until the most recent layer had set, a matter as little as a day or as much as a

1.9. *Demolition for road improvement of the former Hunter's Inn at Week Cross, High Bickington. A cob walled house is revealed behind a traditionally thick coat of lime render.*

few weeks, depending on the weather and the technical performance of the local material. The depths of the 'lifts' or 'raises', often clearly visible in unrendered cob, similarly depended on the nature of the local cob and its propensity to slump or collapse. This system, which was done either with or without shutters, can be regarded as the mainstream technique. There is clear documentary evidence, however, that Devon cob was sometimes erected by building the whole wall at once, using both shuttered and unshuttered techniques. (See, for example, the climbing shuttering method described by C.H. Laycock in 'The Old Devon Farmhouse'.[4])

An unrendered cob wall such as is found in many farm buildings and garden walls offers immense visual pleasure in the coherence of building and landscape, the walls taking up the colours of the ploughed fields and muddy lanes: deep red on the sandstones of central and south Devon and a whole range of cream, buff, yellow, orange and grey on the Culm measures and

1.10. *Higher House, Atherington: structural fracture in cob wall of barn.*

in the cob barn at New Hall Farm, Broadclyst. Newly built cob is still being raised: the bus shelter at Down St Mary was erected in 1978 by traditional methods under the supervision of Mr Alfred Howard. Plans for a cob-built extension to an existing house in a mid Devon village were recently drawn up by Architecton, a Bristol-based firm of architects, and approved by the local planning authority. A cob-walled shelter was erected at Starcross in 1989 under the direction of Larry Keefe of Teignbridge District Council.

Stone and slate

Devon has a highly complex geology (1.11) and it is the variety of local building stones, rather than the predominance of a single high quality stone, that is the most noticeable feature of local building (plate 4). While the larger towns often had access to imported stone, the builders of houses and farm buildings in the countryside often simply opened up an on-site quarry specifically for one building project even if this was only for rubble stone plinths for cob walling. This is a tribute to the availability of some kind of building stone almost everywhere, but the technical excellence of cob as a building material and the indifferent quality of the stone in large areas of the county meant that cob was often used in combination with stone. When not built of cob, the solid walls of rural houses and the side walls of town houses are mostly built of coursed or random rubble with earth mortar using the ubiquitous schists and slatestones of west and north Devon and the South Hams, the limestones of south Devon and the granite of Dartmoor. Often such stonework was rendered and limewashed making it difficult to tell whether it is stone or cob. Solid internal walls are more common than internal timber framing in rural houses in the west and north of the county. Smaller amounts of higher quality stone were used for prestigious display features such as the visible sections of the chimney stack, for door frames and windows and, in towns, for the exposed side walls to the street elevation, which are sometimes corbelled out with the timber jetties.

Ashlar masonry as external walling is comparatively unusual at local level. Granite is most frequently used for this purpose but only around Dartmoor. Its use is especially notable in church

the Devonian slates and shales (plate 3). But on house walls the cob is usually protected by a continuous coating of lime plaster and lime wash. For similar reasons of weather protection, the eaves overhang of thatch is usually impressively and characteristically wide to throw the rainwater off well clear of the wall. Erosion of the wall receiving the worst of the weather is common on unrendered cob walls.

Cob shrinks considerably when it dries which makes it very difficult to repair cob with cob and achieve a proper bond. Hence the traditional method of using rubble stone, brick or more recently concrete blocks in cob wall repair, though this creates even more problems in bonding between such radically different materials. Nevertheless there are some examples of cob buildings which have been gradually completely faced in rubble stone. Cob can be demolished, remixed and reconstructed as was done at the rear wing at Oxenham Farm, Sigford, by Oliver Bosence a few years ago or more recently by the National Trust in the buttresses

houses, the upper-hall houses at Yeo, Chagford and Neadon, Manaton and in some of the grander longhouses like Shilstone, Throwleigh, Hole, Chagford and West Combe, North Bovey and Sanders, Lettaford; in each case ashlar is used for the shippon as well as the house. The great range of other available building stones is also occasionally employed for ashlar walling in smaller rural houses but is more commonly reserved for the particular features already mentioned. There are two very different limestones: the soft creamy-white Cretaceous Beer stone of east Devon and the harder grey Devonian limestone of south Devon. Some of the latter limestones could be polished: the so called Ashburton marble, which is dark grey with pink and white veins, was particularly popular for eighteenth-century fireplace surrounds. There is an even wider choice of sandstones; the yellow/green Salcombe stone from the Upper Greensand in east Devon; the bright red/pink Permian sandstones familiar on the south Devon cliffs; the grey Devonian sandstones of north and south Devon; and, rather less useful as a display stone, the greyish brown Carboniferous sandstone of the Culm measures. Then there are the local specialities like the Upper Greensand churt of east Devon and the Budleigh Salterton pebble beds; the purply volcanic traps of the Exeter, Raddon and Killerton areas; and the greenish metamorphosed tuff giving the distinctive Hurdwick stone of the Tavistock area.[5] Exeter Cathedral is a show case of many of these building stones on a grand scale.

During the medieval period and right down to the nineteenth century, Devon was a major producer of slate, with large quarries in north, west and south Devon. Slate was being exported in quantity from Dartmouth and Totnes from as early as the twelfth and thirteenth centuries, some for building in Exeter and other Devon towns, some for export out of the county to other parts of England and the continent.[6] Only the latter part of this century has Devon been without its own native slate quarry, though large quantities of Welsh and Cornish slates have been imported into the county particularly since the railway network developed in the second half of the nineteenth century. Slate from the Delabole quarry in north Cornwall was used in the construction of Bridgeland Street, Bideford, in the late seventeenth century.

The colour ranges of Devon slates are considerable. Compare for example the west Devon slates: the distinctive brownish colour of Coryton slate (as on part of the roof at Sydenham House) and the greenish/grey slates produced from

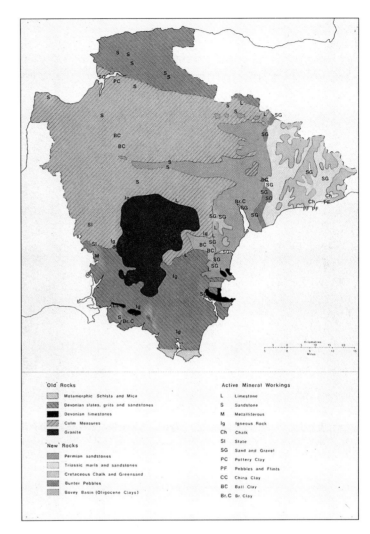

1.11. *Geology of Devon. Geological diversity produces many local building stones. Many are unsuitable for more than rubble walling.*

1.12. 12 North Street, Ashburton
Renewal of the patterned slate cladding (opposite) in 1988 involved (bottom left) carpentry repairs to the timber framed front wall including replacement of the close boarding between the frame members, (middle) nailing the slates to the boards and setting them in lime mortar (bottom right) cutting out the card suite patterns and building up the exact original shapes.

the Mill Hill quarry near Tavistock and which roof so many buildings in that town centre. The lighter greys, greens and blues of the Harbertonford and Ashburton slates can still be seen in quantity in the south Devon towns of Ashburton, Kingsbridge and Totnes, as well as on many a farmstead in south and west Devon.

Varieties of colour and texture were enhanced by the traditional method of laying slates in random widths and diminishing courses, producing both horizontal and vertical variation in the appearance of the roof.[7] Each course is made up of slates of differing widths, while the length of the slates diminishes from the longest at the eaves course to the shortest at the ridge. Whether new laid or covered with lichen and moss such roofs have a visual liveliness and natural beauty which is unique: a world away from the dull mathematical appearance of slate substitutes. One detail of such roofs is worth noting: very often hipped roofs are finished with mitred joints, where the end slates are cut to the angle of the hip laid over lead flashings with no overlaying mortar fillet or ridge tile to cover the tight joints of the slates.

Slate is also used as a wall cladding in south and west Devon and to a lesser extent in north Devon. Sometimes this is part of the original design of the weather proofing of the wall surface, sometimes it is an added protective layer. Small slates in random widths are commonly used for this purpose; while later examples may be nailed to battens, earlier examples are often oak pegged and sometimes set in lime mortar. This slate hanging can be applied to solid and timber-framed walls. At 12 North Street, Ashburton, the seventeenth-century front has boarding fixed between the timber framing which produces a flush surface to which the slates are fixed by this method (1.12). This is one of the two spectacular examples in Ashburton of patterned slate cladding. The first and second storeys of the street elevation are clad in very small slates into which the geometric patterns of the card suites – hearts, spades, diamonds and clubs – are incised and coloured. This has recently had to be meticulously renewed by Oliver Bosence, a local builder specializing in such traditional methods. No. 33 East Street has similar small slates but shaped individually to a round profile giving an overall impression of fish scales.

1.13. *Slate techniques*
(Top) random widths and diminishing courses with mitred hips (Hemerdon)
(Bottom) patterned slate cladding (Ashburton)

1.14. *The Old Manor, Talaton. A brick cladding was added c. 1700 to a late medieval house, but only to the principal elevations.*

1.15. *Small yellow/buff 'dutch' bricks of the seventeenth century at Topsham below later and larger red bricks*

Brick and tile

Although it arrived relatively late, brick has a claim to be one of the significant historic building materials of the county. In the fifteenth to eighteenth centuries it is, however, much more of an urban than a rural material: it remains a rarity in the countryside and even then is used more for chimney stacks (e.g. Westacott, North Tawton and Churchgate Cottages, East Budleigh) and ovens than for walling. But there are some good late seventeenth- and eighteenth-century brick-walled farmhouses scattered randomly over the county. A good north Devon example is the brick front of Rookabear just south-east of Barnstaple: this has a plastered brick fireplace dated 1630, which makes it one of the earliest dated brick houses in Devon. Examples are more frequently found to the east of Exeter, for example Harris's Farm, Talaton, which is dated 1673. At the neighbouring property, the Old Manor, Talaton, the medieval house received brick front cladding to the front and side elevations in the early eighteenth century (1.14). Deep in west Devon was Combepark, Broad-woodwidger, an early eighteenth-century brick house on a double-pile plan sadly demolished for the Roadford Reservoir in 1987. The bricks for this remote house may have been produced from a local brickworks, since they occur in local farm buildings as well; perhaps a reminder that many local brickworks once existed in Devon which accounts for the rather sporadic distribution of brick buildings until the advent of the major brickworks of the nineteenth century.

In town buildings there is much more striking evidence. Some of the earliest brick seems to have been imported from the continent (probably from Holland) through Topsham and Dartmouth and is found as a walling material in the seventeenth-century houses of these towns. These bricks are small, thin and buff coloured, quite different from the late eighteenth-century bricks of Exeter's Georgian buildings which are larger, and coloured deeper red (1.15). Some Regency brick buildings in Sidmouth are plastered and rendered suggesting that brick was not considered a suitable material for display at that period: instead, like many later and more modest buildings throughout Devon villages and towns, the smooth render is lined out in slight vertical and horizontal markings to simulate the appearance of stonework.

Occasional houses are tuck pointed, a relatively late deceit to give the impression of mathematically precise high-quality brickwork: this is achieved by colouring over the whole surface of both bricks and mortar joints and then applying thin vertical and horizontal lines in white line putty to simulate the brickwork joints.[8] There is a recently restored example at 61 Fore Street, Totnes. An even rarer brickwork deceit is the use of mathematical tiles which are special tiles made to fix onto the wall surface so as to simulate the appearance of high quality brickwork.[9] There are examples in red at the Red House, Bridgeland Street, Bideford and in yellow/buff at the Law Chambers, Silver Street and Victoria House, Castle Street, Axminster. On a grander scale they are used to face Nutwell Court, Lympstone.

Although outside our period, an honourable mention must be made of the pale yellow bricks from Kingsteignton in south Devon and Peters Marland in north Devon which are displayed in so many nineteenth-century buildings. Ilfracombe is perhaps the most striking example of the consistent use of such local bricks, for example for the later Victorian development of the villas of the Torrs Estate.[10]

Red clay tiles deserve a brief mention because they are a significant roofing material particularly for traditional farm buildings, being especially frequent in the east of the county towards the Somerset border. This reflects the proximity to the Bridgewater area where firms like Browns made tiles for export to Brittany as well as throughout the South West, especially in the nineteenth century.

Lime

Lime is fundamental to traditional building technology. It is the basis of soft lime mortars for stonework, of lime renders for simple but effective weather proofing and of lime wash to protect and colour the surfaces of walls and ceilings. It is even used for flooring as lime ash, a finish as hard as modern cement. In combination with cob plaster, it is the raw material for decorative plasterwork. These traditional lime-based components of local building technology are immensely tolerant and adaptable, allowing both moisture and air to pass throughout them and thus allowing the building to breathe, moisten and dry out naturally, as well as coping with the inevitable and essential microscopic movements of the structure. When these lime finishes are combined with cob or rubble stone walls with earth mortar without damp proofing courses and cavities, the result is a completely different moisture regime for the building when compared to modern construction.

It is because lime offers an appropriate technology for the traditional structure that interest in revising the techniques of lime mortar, render and lime wash has grown rapidly.[11] The most useable form of lime for these purposes is lime putty formed by the slaking (i.e. the addition of water) of natural lump lime. This process is dramatic with the mixture boiling furiously at very high temperatures for a brief time. After settlement putty lime can be cut into blocks and stored for use. For lime washes the putty lime is mixed with tallow and whey or, more easily obtainable, glue size and natural dyes to produce beautiful colours and textures to complement both interior and exterior surfaces. For a recent comprehensive scheme of lime washing it is worth looking at the National Trust's Killerton Estate near Exeter: here farmsteads and cottages as well as virtually the whole of the historic centre of the village of Broadclyst are all now resplendent in a wide range of yellowy, creamy, pale and red lime washes (plate 1). The finished walls have a gently mottled nature rather than the bland uniformity produced by modern cement based paints.

For mortars, plasters and renders varying degrees of aggregate are added depending on the required finish. An external render will usually have a finish in which the aggregate is still visible but not so aggressively rough that anyone brushing against it will be cut. This will be a finishing coat on top of a dubbing-out coat and will have been applied by throwing the lime render onto the wall. For a text book example, visit Torbryan church where, in early 1988, the tower was completely re-rendered in lime and sand and then limewashed under the supervision of John Schofield of Architecton of Bristol, (contractors Dart and Francis of Crediton). Both internally and externally lime plaster and lime render take up the natural gentle undulations of walls and ceilings. It is equally capable when mixed with fine sand and animal hair of producing a soft smooth finish and, with cob plaster, is the basic material of the Devonshire plasterwork tradition of the sixteenth and seventeenth centuries described and illustrated in Chapter 7.

As for lime ash floors, *The Builders' Dictionary* of 1734[12] gives four recipes for use in 'plain country habitations' quoted below in full; these indicate the range of materials and techniques used in what are now generally known as lime ash floors but which might perhaps be more accurately described as composition floors.

Take two Thirds of Lime, and one of Coal Ashes well-fitted, with a small Quantity of loamy Clay; mix the Whole that you intend to use together, and temper it well with Water; making it up into a Heap, let it lie a Week or ten Days, in which Time it will mellow and digest: Then temper it well over again, and be sure that your Quantity of Water does not exceed, but rather that it may obtain a mellow Softness and Toughness from Labour: Then heap it up again for three or four Days, and repeat the Tempering very high, till it becomes smooth and yielding though and glewy.

Then the Ground being levelled, lay your Floor therewith about two and a half or three Inches thick, making it smooth with a Trowel: the hotter the Season is, the better; and when it is throughly dry'd it will continue Time out of Mind.

This makes the best Floors for Houses, especially for Malt-Houses; but as for as those who cannot get there Materials, or go to the Charge of them, they may take of clayey Loam and new soft Horse-Dung one Third, with a small Quantity of Coal Ashes, if they can be had, and temper thereafter the aforementioned Manner and lay the Floor with the Stuff three or four inches thick, smooth and even, which will cement, become hard, strong and durable, being done in a hot and dry season; good for Cottages, Barns, and other small Houses.

But if any would have more beautiful Floors than these, they must lay their Floors even, smooth, and fine, either with the first or last mentioned Flooring; then take Lime made of Rag-Stones, and temper it with a little Whites of Eggs, the more Eggs the better, to a very high pitch, with which cover your Floor about a quarter or half an Inch thick, before the under Flooring be too dry, that they may well incorporate together: This being well done, and throughly dry, if sometimes rubbed over with Mops or Cloths, with a little Oil thereon, it will look very beautiful and transparent, as if it were polished Metal or Glass, provided the Eggs and Lime were throughly tempered, and otherwise well performed. Sir Hugh Plat gives us a Receipt for making an artificial Composition where with to make smooth, glittering, and hard Floors; and which may also serve for plastering of Walls.

1.16. *Upcott, near Dolton. Wheat reed thatch with a plain ridge, the mainstream Devon thatching tradition*

1.17. *Bill Hammond thatching a barn roof at Newhouse, Ashreigny*

Ox Blood and fine Clay tempered together, he says, makes the finest Floor in the Worls; and that this Mixture laid in any Floor or Wall, will become a very strong and binding Substance.

Thatch

Great sweeps of grey thatch running over gently undulating roof lines with deep eaves overhanging lime-washed walls are one of the visual delights of Devon (1.16). Such thatched roofs are also likely to be of considerable historic importance because thatch was the roofing material of so much of Devon, urban and rural, from the fifteenth to nineteenth centuries. It gradually receded in the towns in the wake of disastrous fires. Far from being a temporary roofing material, Devon thatch is a powerful witness to the longevity of this historic natural product with hundreds of houses having their original thatch in the lowest layers of the roof surviving from as far back as the fifteenth century.

A properly maintained thatched roof needs its ridge renewed regularly and its main slopes recoated occasionally but the under thatch can lie undisturbed, sometimes building up to great thicknesses. It is still possible to look into the roof space of a small Devon house and see not only medieval roof carpentry but medieval thatch as well, often very heavily sooted from the open hall phase (plate 2). Even where there are medieval smoke louvres, the extent of the smoke blackening is still impressive. Very often the whole roof is in a condition that it was left when the chambers were ceiled, in perhaps the seventeenth century, with the original riven battens and hazel ties still perfectly preserved. An outstanding example is the roof at Lower Chilverton, Coldridge. Such early thatch may be laid directly onto wattles instead of rafters (as at Townsend Farm, Stockland) or on an under thatch layer of heather, gorse or broom as at East Down Farm, Dunsford. Even with later seventeenth-century and eighteenth-century thatch there may be no purlins or rafters, but simply wide thatching battens laid between the principals.

Rye, water reed and combed wheat reed are all of authentic local provenance in Devon. Water reed was a naturally available crop in a county like Devon with so many extensive river estuaries. But it was combed wheat reed that predominated until the recent large-scale importation of continental water reed, the latter gaining popularity because of its greater longevity under modern growing conditions. Although this is not the place to rehearse the arguments about this subject, it is worth stressing that thatching is a local building craft, not a uniform technique which can be indiscriminately applied all over the country to provide a superficially pretty appearance to old houses. For example, the water reed roof is much coarser in texture and stiffer in appearance compared to the softness and smoothness of wheat reed, Add a thick incised patterned ridge, and the gentle simplicity of the Devon roof has been replaced by something quite different and much more assertive. [15] Those thatchers who are aware that the combed wheat reed tradition is threatened deserve encouragement and support in growing and using strains of wheat (e.g. the Maris varieties) that can be commercially viable again. In this way the combed wheat reed tradition of Devon thatching can stand as a symbol, both of hope for the future, and also of the fragility of all these local building methods and materials: something 'nearly the same' is definitely not the same as 'the real thing'.

2.1. *Ashwell, Dolton. A seventeenth-century farmhouse standing isolated in the landscape, but enclosed by its own farmyard buildings.*

2

Farmhouse Building Traditions

PETER CHILD

D evon is rich in old farmhouses scattered thickly over most of the county. They are essentially traditional buildings, constructed of local materials in a limited variety of types evolving over the centuries to serve changing social needs. Their systematic investigation, particularly in recent years, enables an overall picture of their evolution to be compiled which this paper attempts to outline. By necessity, great generalizations are made and exceptions to them will be readily found; nevertheless, a consistent pattern can be observed by those interested enough to probe the fascinating and under-explored wealth of historic buildings represented by Devon's farmhouses.

The local background

Above a certain social level, building traditions take on a national rather than local form, so that the houses of the gentry in style and plan and often in materials did not differ substantially throughout England. On the other hand farmhouses until relatively recent times were designed essentially on a traditional and local basis, this being considered more important than the requirements of national architectural fashion. Consequently each region shows a distinctive type of farmhouse. The one found in Devon is not exclusive to the county as it belongs to a

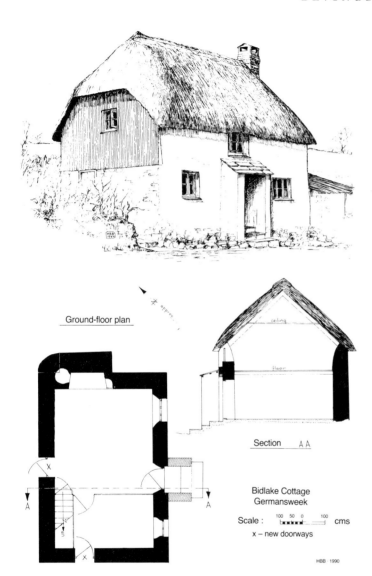

Ground-floor plan

Section A A

Bidlake Cottage
Germansweek

Scale : 100 50 0   100 cms

x – new doorways

HBB · 1990

2.2. Bidlake Cottage, Germansweek, Cob and thatched cottages similar to this can be seen anywhere in Devon. They are difficult to date because of their simplicity but are probably not older than the eighteenth century, and were constructed for labourers or artisans rather than for farmers. Only one of the two ground-floor rooms is heated (with a bread oven in the fireplace); the other was a bedroom or storeroom, the basic character of such cottages is soon eroded by modernization and extensions.

type which has parallels occurring throughout England and Wales at certain periods, but is a version of this type which has its own quite distinctive features. The buildings to be described were not erected by or for those belonging to the lowest social classes but for the comparatively prosperous independent or tenant farmer. Labourers' cottages were so insubstantially built that only those of comparatively recent date have survived (2.2); Vancouver in 1808 describes those of Chilworthy as consisting only of 'three mud walls and a hedge bank'[1] and such flimsy structures might have stood only for the length of a single generation. Indeed, the likelihood of the survival of a building is directly related to its size and substance which, in turn, is related to the wealth of its builder.

The medieval manorial system in Devon compared with many other parts of England allowed a larger proportion of freehold land owners[2] and the three-life lease system of tenancy for those who were not freeholders, which became prevalent from the sixteenth century onwards,[3] was relatively generous to the tenant, enabling single families to retain long occupation of single holdings. Both these factors encouraged spending on farmhouses; an insecure tenant will obviously be reluctant to put his capital into building. Agriculture flourished in the sixteenth and seventeenth centuries and the combined result is a legacy of thousands of fine traditional buildings. These are scattered evenly across the landscape in single farmsteads or small hamlets; the nucleated village with several farms concentrated together is exceptional in Devon (plate 6). The reasons for this dispersed settlement pattern are complex but partly result from the same relatively relaxed medieval tenurial system which has provided such a wealth of early houses.[4] The consequence is a countryside where you may find fine traditional farmhouses around the corner of any lane.

Farmhouse plan forms

These farmhouses divide into two separate types. The first is one where cattle are sheltered under the same roof as their owners (the 'longhouse'); the second is one where the whole house is used solely for domestic purposes. Confusingly, the plan form of the two types is virtually identical, consisting of three rooms divided by a passage across the width of the building. Despite this similarity, the origins of the two types are very different. On the one hand the house shared by animals and humans is a form found continuously in European prehistory, and arguably the Devon form descends from this long traditional line. On the other hand the ubiquitous alternative solely domestic type appears to have its origins only in the Middle Ages. It is significant that long-houses survive only as standing buildings in the harsher and remoter parts of Devon, namely Dartmoor and Exmoor, and nationally are confined to the highland parts of the United Kingdom. In the more affluent and accessible lowland areas of the county the longhouse is virtually absent among surviving farmhouses, giving way entirely to houses designed solely for human occupation. This is not to say that there were never longhouses in these lower parts, because, as elsewhere in England, these may well be revealed by future archaeological excavation. What it does mean is that at a threshold in time at which houses of sufficient substance were constructed to have survived to the present day, the builders' wish was not to carry on with the ancient traditional form but to turn to a very different functional concept. Being the products of a single society and because of the constraints of vernacular materials, externally and even internally the buildings may look very similar but there was a fundamental difference in how their builders conceived the use of the two types. Since longhouses are of such special interest in

Devon a separate chapter upon them is included in this volume and this chapter will concern itself only with the solely domestic form.

The cross-passage house

This alternative type is believed to have originated nationally at a higher social level than that of the structures with which this paper is concerned. The traditional Devon farmhouse copies, in a much reduced scale, the principles of the plan of the mansions of the upper classes repeating, in a size dependant on the builder's wealth or ambitions, a consistent three-unit house plan with two rooms on one side of a cross-passage and one on the other (2.3). The passage had an external door at the either end and abutted on one side the major living room of the houses, commonly called the 'hall', and on the other a room for 'service' functions usually connected with food processing or storage. Conventionally, the hall side is referred to as being 'above' the passage, the service side as 'below'. On the opposite side of the hall from the passage lay an inner room which usually seems to have functioned as accommodation rather than for service. The

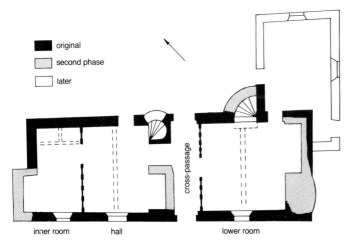

original
second phase
later

inner room   hall   cross-passage   lower room

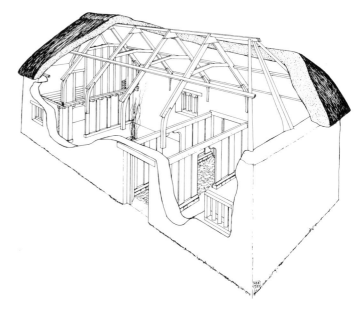

2.3. (Right) a part-floored medieval farmhouse. The first floor of the upper end is jettied into an open hall with its central fireplace. Head-height screens divide the hall from the cross-passage and the service room in the lower end. The thatched roof is supported on jointed cruck trusses with hip posts at either end. (Left) ground-floor plan of a three-roomed cross-passage house (Lower Lye, Stockland).

allocation of specific functions to the separate rooms of this consistent plan is fraught with problems (particularly in view of the destruction of the vital documentary evidence, which could have been provided by the probate inventories destroyed in the bombing of Exeter), but it is possible to make some assumptions, both from analogy with the greater buildings aped by the farms and from better-documented parts of the country.

The hall in particular must be regarded as the principal room of the house, both from its greater size and from the more lavish decoration given to its fittings. Significantly, it was often the only room originally with a hearth. The inner room leading off it may as commonly have been a bedroom (a 'chamber') or a private living room (a 'parlour'), but with the creation of more bedrooms on the upper floor the latter function became more common, although its lack of a fireplace in some instances caused it to be down-graded to a more utilitarian purpose, such as a dairy. In any event, it seems that this room was regarded as the least essential of the three, as a small but significant number of two-room cross-passage houses exist (Luggs Farm, Membury). Two-room houses with a cross-passage at one end below the hall also occur (Higher Furze, Filleigh) but are even rarer. It also seems that some early houses had unusually long halls which were later sub-divided to provide an inner room after the standard fashion (Middlemoor, Sowton).[5] Single-room houses of any great age are very rare, although there are a handful (Monkstone, Brent Tor).

The identification of rooms is not made easier by the changes

2.4. Stud-and-panel partitions at Lower Chilverton, Coldridge, which originally stood as a free-standing screen within an open medieval house. The ceiling was inserted in the seventeenth century at a higher level than the screen and the resulting gap has a plastered infill.

of terminology over time or the use of different words to describe the same room (just as we today interchange 'lounge' and 'living room'); a seventeenth-century inventory description, for instance, calls one room 'the hall or parlour'. The function of the hall as the house's dining room is commonly shown by the recorded presence (in inventories) of tables and benches there, as well as eating utensils, and it is reasonable to assume that before the seventeenth century its hearth was where the household's cooking took place, at least where there was no separately built kitchen outside the house – an arrangement which has been discovered, although its original frequency is hard to ascertain (Damage Barton, Mortehoe). It would appear that at a later stage, with an increased desire to divide domestic functions into separate specific rooms, the lower room was turned into a proper kitchen, as large fireplaces suitable for cooking occur here from the early seventeenth century. The earlier storage and food processing nature (particularly dairying and brewing) of this lower end, for which purposes it might be divided into two rooms longitudinally, (Cordwents, Halberton) then became squeezed out into smaller additional rooms in freestanding outbuildings or incorporated in extensions.

Development of the farmhouse

The evolution of this three-room-and-cross-passage type from its earliest form is largely concerned with the process of sub-dividing the house into a greater number of compartments, both vertically and horizontally, and by the addition of end extensions, wings and lean-tos. Changing social priorities altered the farmhouse over the centuries from a barn-like structure open to the roof trusses, and with minimal divisions, into a two-storey edifice clearly divided into a number of rooms in the manner of a house as we conceive it today. Remarkably, the basic ground plan was retained throughout these changes until ousted by the spread of national styles in the eighteenth century.

The open-hall house

First in this classification is the basic medieval house, single-storeyed, but often of nearly equivalent height to a two-storey building. Divisions into rooms were made by low partitions of head-height only, above which the smoke of the chimneyless hearth located in the hall could eddy uninterruptedly, staining the rafters of the roof and the underside of the thatch black with congealed soot. This staining and encrustation (resembling the coating of the inside of a chimney) is crucial for the identification of these medieval houses, for it often remains the only evidence of this primary phase, otherwise completely obscured by later alterations. The degree of smoke-blackening is often impressive, partly perhaps because commonly no aperture was provided for the smoke to escape, so that it had to percolate through and under the thatch. Even where smoke louvres in the roof have been identified (West Clatworthy, Filleigh,[6] and Middle Clyst William, Plymtree: plate 2) the smoke-blackening is not visibly less. Townsend Farm, Stockland, has five bays (the intervals between the roof trusses) all showing evidence by smoke-blackening of having originally been one continuous open space. Although often no evidence of the nature of the original low partitions survives, in some instances it is clear that they were elaborate timber screens of a type which continued to be used until the late seventeenth century in fully floored houses. That some of these screens originally stood free within the barn-like open space of the hall house is evidenced by the rough way in which the first floor wall is tacked onto them rather than being properly framed into it in the normal manner (Lower Chilverton, Coldridge (2.4)).[8] In other instances the partitions would have been simpler

2.5. *A sixteenth-century open hall which has survived unfloored at the Manor House barn, Cheriton Fitzpaine*

2.6. *Interior of open hall in Elizabethan times with a central open hearth. The jetty of the upper room (reached by a ladder stair) forms a canopy over the bench against the screen at the upper end. The roof trusses are arch-braced and the underside of the thatch is lined with wattles.*

framed or solid walls, almost impossible to identify after subsequent alteration.

Some single-storey houses had original partitions reaching the full height of the house, sometimes with open hearths in the rooms on either side (Middle Clyst William, Plymtree); more commonly, they divided an unheated area of the house from a heated one, particularly the lower service end from the hall and cross-passage. The smoke-blackening of the trusses on one side of a partition but not on the other is a good indication of this (Rudge, Morchard Bishop[9]). Such original full height partitions may be indicated by the employment of 'closed' trusses, that is pairs of rafters linked by a tie-beam at eaves level which held vertical studs between which wattle or lathe and daub infill was inserted to form the internal wall. 'Open' trusses in contrast had no cross-member, save possibly for a high collar, and in medieval houses these provided the effect of unbroken spaciousness sought after by the property owner at the expense of convenience and floorspace. Open and closed trusses in themselves do not necessarily indicate a medieval date, as this structural system remained in use even in later two-storey houses, where open trusses continued to be used where no internal partition was required.

The roof structure of the open-hall house was fully visible and consequently was constructed to a more than simply functional standard in most instances. Although Devon roofs are not as generously timbered or elaborately decorated as in some parts of England they are nevertheless of a generally high quality and display very characteristic regional features, in particular the use of the jointed-cruck truss. The pre-eminence of the hall amongst the rooms of the house is often emphasized by the use of a more elaborate truss perhaps using braces to the collar to provide the appearance of a Gothic arch, or by the use of curved and sometimes cusped wind-braces in the plane of the roof slope between the purlins and rafters (plate 2). Devon roof types are more fully described in Chapter 1 of this volume.

The two-storey house

At a date which cannot be pin-pointed, but probably in the mid sixteenth century, the farmer began to insert floors into his previously open house so as to form an upper storey, in order to provide more accommodation. Wholly two-storey houses did exist before this date, but these were in a minority, particularly at lower social levels, compared to the fully open-hall house type. From this time, the trend was either to modify these to provide two storeys or to build new houses in this manner, so that the single-storey house became progressively more obsolete. This was a national change; it occurs throughout England in this period and reflects a new attitude toward house construction. It was no longer considered necessary for a man to demonstrate his status by the enclosure of a large open space; such status could be achieved by the more elaborate furniture and decoration of several rooms. Such sub-division reflects a change in social attitudes with a greater emphasis on privacy and convenience than before. Good farming profits at this time no doubt accelerated the process of change but were not in themselves the reason for it. Indeed the size of the earlier houses is quite comparable with their successors and many could be divided comfortably into two storeys without raising the roof. In other instances the inserted upper rooms were very low and roofs have subsequently been raised to accommodate them more satisfactorily. Houses were not necessarily made two-storey at one stroke; the process was commonly achieved in stages, partly perhaps indicating a reluctance to abandon completely the traditional open house and partly for the technical reason that the flooring of an open hall with its open hearth necessitated automatically the provision of an expensive chimney-stack. Thus, partial flooring only of the house took place, leaving the hall as the last part to remain open before the creation of a totally two-storey house. In Devon the manner in which this was done often took an idiosyncratic form, with the ends of the inserted floor carried forward over the ground floor partition so that the first floor wall was set forward from it in the manner of jettied front walls of contemporary urban building; such a device has hence been called an 'internal jetty' (2.6, 2.7). This construction appears to have been purely decorative, the exposed joist ends often being chamfered and stopped; when constructed at the upper end of the hall it formed a sort of canopy over the 'high table' but it was also sometimes formed over the lower end and in some instances, at both ends, as at Little Rull, Cullompton. An internal jetty could be placed over an existing low partition (Priesthall, Kentisbeare[11]) or inserted as a completely new feature (Middlemoor, Sowton[5]), or be in a house's primary design (Glebe House, Whitestone).[12]

2.7. An internal jetty at the Old Manor, Talaton, with the joists of the inner room carried over the screen to project into the originally open hall

The survival of such jetties (quite frequent in east and central Devon) is a certain indication that part at least of a house was, at one stage, open to the roof. In fact, it is considerably easier to identify part-floored houses with this feature, than those which employed a flush full-height partition for the same purpose. In these latter buildings the evidence will lie in the extent of smoke-blackening of the roof trusses and on clues provided in inconsistencies in the decoration and structural relationships of ground floor ceiling beams.

Inevitably, the insertion of floors necessitated the provision of fireplaces and stacks to control the smoke which previously had drifted into the roof space. Some houses anticipated this insertion by substituting fireplaces within the open hall for the open hearth, but generally both the works were carried out simultaneously. The location of the fireplace within the hall in this final stage is generally consistent (2.8, plates 5, 7); it most usually backs onto the cross-passage nearest the front entrance along the short axis of the house (an 'axial' stack). The most common alternative to this position (2.9) is the front wall of the house with the stack then proudly dominating this elevation (a 'lateral'

stack). Such a position is a feature particularly found in the South West and seems to have been intended to impress the visitor at the expense of heat conservation. Stacks and fireplaces set in the inner and back wall of the hall are also found exceptionally. Fireplaces are not always found in the inner room; in the upper chambers they occur at least from the late sixteenth century. As befits perhaps the most important feature of the room, the lintels and jambs are commonly moulded (2.10), while the occasional decoration of the inner and back faces of fireplaces (albeit somewhat impractically) with patterned black and white plasterwork seem to be a seventeenth century speciality of the county.[15]

The hall's pre-eminence among the rooms of the house is often emphasized by its more elaborate decoration in the form of moulded beams and panelled walls. Applied square panelling is found from the sixteenth and seventeenth centuries, but most common are oak stud and panel ('plank and muntin') partitions across the width of the house, at the same time structural and decorative (2.4.). These originate probably in the fifteenth century as low partitions in open halls and continue in use in two-storey houses until the end of the seventeenth century. Between a plain cill beam and a moulded head beam are set a row of close-set studs each slotted down the side to take a substantial plank. The studs are chamfered and stopped and the position of the latter (if relatively high off the floor) can indicate that there was originally a bench set against the panelling, usually at the high end the wall if this has not actually survived (Poltimore Farmhouse, Farway[14]). In late examples of these screens the chamfering is replaced by scratch moulding. One or more doorways were integrated in these panelled partitions; these have shaped heads, shouldered (Cleavehanger, Nymet Rowland[15]) or arched, sometimes with carved spandrels. Ceiling beams in the principal room are almost always decorated at least with chamfers and stops, and commonly with moulding of different elaboration; roll mouldings of the sixteenth century are replaced by the characteristic quarter-round ('ovolo') mould of the seventeenth century. Even the joists can be moulded or chamfered on occasion, while particularly lavish, and generally sixteenth-century in date, are ceilings of intersecting beams, often heavily moulded, forming a grid pattern under exposed joists running in alternate directions in each panel (7.1) provide an even more striking effect (South Yard, Rose Ash[16]). Much of this timberwork seems to have been painted with

2.8. Lower Lye, Stockland. The axial stack inserted into a medieval house can be seen immediately above the cross-passage.

2.9. A farmhouse with inserted lateral stack: Lower Chilverton, Coldridge

patterns although usually only tiny traces now remain. This form of ornament together with that of the fine moulded plaster ceilings found throughout the county (and which conversely do not seem to have been painted) are treated separately in Chapter 7 because of the national significance of the Devon plasterwork tradition.

Staircases were located inconsistently. Part-floored houses sometimes only had a ladder stair rising from the open hall to an opening in the face of the first floor partition (Livenhayes, Stockland) but early staircases are often contained in rounded projections usually on the back wall within which is a newel stair commonly with solid timber wedge-shaped treads. These stairs sometimes lead to little lobbies at their head from which two doors would lead to separate rooms. Until a relatively late date upper chambers usually were interconnecting but a seventeenth-century corridor arrangement is known at Higher Rixdale, Dawlish. From the seventeenth century also are sometimes found fully framed staircases in rear projections as at Great Moor, Sowton (2.11.)[17], but often it is very hard to ascertain the position of the original staircase as these were replaced in the eighteenth and nineteenth centuries by framed staircases in the

2.10. Beerstone fireplace in an upper chamber at Poltimore Farm, Farway. It is dated 1583, presumably the year when the medieval open hall was floored.

2.11. Projecting rear stair turret of the seventeenth century at Woodland, Yeoford

2.12. Projecting hall bay at Higher Furze, Chittlehampton. This seventeenth-century house is unusual in not originally having a service end below the cross-passage.

hall or kitchen (or both where a servants' backstair was required) at a point in time when the open spaciousness of these rooms was no longer valued. Blocked doorways in first-floor outside walls may indicate the position of an old stair but may alternatively have belonged to a garderobe (lavatory) shaft.[18]

Farmhouses could be extended in various ways. In north and west Devon 'hall bays' are occasionally found when the front wall of the hall is brought forward to emphasize the importance of this room (Higher Furze and Dinnacombes, Chittlehampton: 2.12[19]). In the seventeenth century two-storey porches over the entrance were fashionable (Comfort House, Bradninch or Langford Court, Cullompton: 2.13). These were prestigious constructions, sometimes dated and initialled, and often of timber-framed construction – a unique external technique for Devon's rural buildings. Rear wings are not uncommon additions, also of the seventeenth century, often with a dairy under a bed chamber (Middlemoor, Sowton). However, full crosswings are very rare (Fishleigh Barton, Tavistock[20]).

The most common extension of all, which can be found almost without exception on the traditional farmhouse, is the rear lean-to or 'outshot', single-storeyed and roofed either continuously with the main slope or from a point below the eaves. Outshots can run along the entire length of a house or only part of it, or be on the end walls. They invariably reflect an addition to the service

rooms, and this humble function tends to deprive them of datable decorative details. However, they are practically always additions rather than original features, which indicates that they generally post-date the traditional style, although there is one medieval example at Yeo Farmhouse, Mariansleigh, and a few seventeenth-century examples are known (Luggs Farm, Membury).

The extension of houses by outshots or wings did not, of course, preclude simply enlarging the house at either of its ends. This happened commonly at all periods and is often most easily observed in the variation of roof trusses of different dates and, less certainly, by the presence of solid internal walls, previously external. Such longitudinal extension was constructionally easy, but produced an inconvenient arrangement of rooms, with as many as five in a line as well as the cross-passage.

Dating

Ascribing convincingly precise dates to these traditional houses is difficult. It is assumed that houses constructed either completely or partly open to the roof are 'medieval' in period and this should

2.13. *A timber-framed entrance porch at Langford Court, Cullompton, dating from the seventeenth century*

be before *c.* 1550. How much before 1550 is almost impossible to say, although dates as early as the thirteenth and fourteenth centuries have been quite convincingly claimed for Pilliven, Witheridge,[21] and Bury Barton, Lapford.[22] Generally, however, the lack of readily datable features defeats attempts to establish whether other hall houses are this early or not, and the day must, therefore, be awaited when scientific techniques such as tree-ring dating are more readily available. With sixteenth-century and post-medieval houses, the position is a little better as beam and panel mouldings show more evolution, but stylistic details were long-lasting and often the ascription of dates is more inspired by intuition, based on experience, than by scientific fact. Building materials, moreover, did not change significantly over the centuries; similarly the jointed-cruck truss lasts from almost the earliest houses to the later seventeenth century.

The final phase

The dominance of the three-room-and-cross-passage house begins to decline in the seventeenth century and traditional forms from elsewhere in the country appear. In particular there are

2.14. South Coombe, Witheridge. A late seventeenth-century lobby-entry house. The stack can be seen rising directly behind the main entrance.

scattered examples of houses entered not through a cross-passage but by a lobby in front of a central stack, serving rooms on either side (2.14). This is the prevalent later type of vernacular house in eastern England but despite its practical design, it never achieved much popularity in Devon. Some of these lobby-entry houses were completely new-built especially in eastern Devon (Houndsmoor, Uplowman) but others (Higher Barnes, Wiggaton) were open halls into which the stack was inserted in this position, blocking previous cross-passage arrangements. Another late variant form are houses with unheated central rooms (Burnthouse, Otterton), perhaps used as dairies, as in Dorset, where the type is relatively common.[25] The search in the seventeenth century for a plan form to serve changing domestic and social requirements is well illustrated by the farmhouses of Ottery Road, Otterton, where along a two-mile stretch of road there are seven farmhouses with different plan types either modifed or newly built at this period. The cross-passage is still found in all of them but variations include the central unheated dairy at Burnthouse; the inclusion of a staircase in the dairy outshot at Passaford and within an added parlour wing at Pitson; the insertion of service rooms behind the hall and kitchen but within the main structure of the house at Pavers; and the placing of the hall stack in the wall facing the cross-passage at Smiths, with a dairy beyond it.

All these plan types were still fundamentally linear in form and were shortly to be superceded by a national style of house soon to become ubiquitous in Devon and the rest of England where a 'classical' desire for a balanced design led to a plan with the placing of equally-sized and fenestrated rooms symmetrically on either side of a central entrance and hallway, from which the staircase rose as an important feature. The symmetry was emphasized by stacks at each gable end. At a lower social level these houses remained of single-room depth, usually with a continuous rear outshot, but the double-depth house was normal for larger farms and for smaller ones from the mid-nineteenth century onwards. Other 'Georgian' features, such as sash windows, became common and frequently earlier traditional buildings adopted such details disguising their older cores, even to the extent of imposing external symmetry on a basically asymmetrical plan. New 'national' materials appear too, particularly Cornish and Welsh slates and brick, gradually ousting thatch, cob and stone. Nonetheless, even these later buildings retained some local flavour, but one which diminished by degrees, so that today, for better or worse, one can only detect the smallest differences between the more recent buildings of Devon and those of any other county.

This essay is an amended version of one originally published in 1978. Since then the study of Devon farmhouses has been advanced by various researches which have tended to consolidate earlier conclusions rather than altering them in any radical way. What is however now available which was not in 1978 are the results of the survey carried out by Architecton in 1984–1987 to revise the Lists of Buildings of Special Architectural or Historic Interest on behalf of English Heritage. Because this was so thoroughly conducted it is likely that the vast majority of significant traditional buildings in three-quarters of the county have been identified and described in detail in the new lists which are publicly accessible. As a result it is potentially possible for the researcher to draw statistical and distributional con-clusions which simply were not feasible previously. This enormous amount of available information awaits compilation and sorting; when this task has been achieved the study of traditional architecture in Devon will be much advanced. Not only will this enable a greater perspective on a fascinating aspect of local history but it will help in the appreciation of these houses as historic structures whose particular character must be considered in the continuing pressure for change and moderniza-tion. The Listing survey would not claim to be exhaustive; virtually any traditional farmhouse needs hours of study to be properly comprehended and often building works expose completely new aspects of its development previously completely concealed. In the field of written records too, the detailed economic background has yet to be elucidated in relation to the agricultural and tenurial systems which provided the surplus which, in turn, paid for the construction of what are very substantial vernacular buildings. The material is plentiful and could not be more visible; its examination as a fundamental part of local history is vital.

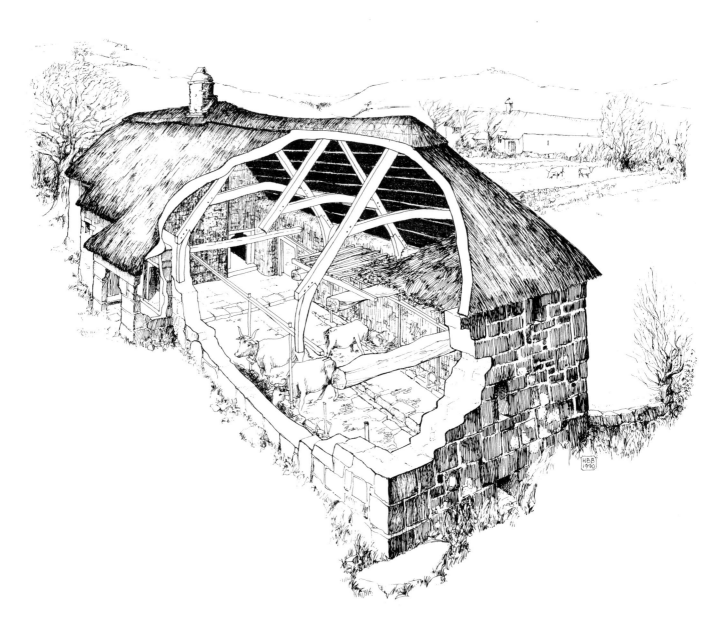

3.1. *Reconstruction drawing of a late-medieval longhouse seen from the shippon end, based on Sanders, Lettaford. Note the cows tethered to the lateral walls.*

3

The Longhouse

PETER BEACHAM

When an old Devon farmhouse is put up for sale more often than not the estate agent's particulars will describe such a property as 'a superb example of a Devon longhouse'. Though a tribute to the continuing popular appreciation of this Devon house type, such a description is unlikely to be accurate. Technically speaking, a longhouse is a dual purpose building type providing human and animal shelter under a common roof. The vast majority of Devon farmhouses of the fifteenth to eighteenth centuries are not, nor ever were, such dual purpose buildings but houses constructed on the two or three room cross-passage form which never contained animal shelter.

Now that the study of local building traditions in Great Britain and elsewhere has developed so rapidly, we can see the Devon longhouse in a better perspective as but one of our local building types which is both scarce (there are less than 125 examples surviving and less than twenty-five with the animal shelter unaltered) and remarkably restricted in its distribution (standing longhouses are almost unknown in the rest of southern England). Nevertheless it deserves special attention because it is a survivor of an early house type of national, indeed international, interest and because its relationship to other vernacular house types is intriguing if problematic. Unless its specialness is more widely recognized as a matter of urgency we will lose for ever a rich cultural resource of Devon history. So we need to ask what a longhouse is, where it is to be found, how old it is and how it developed in Devon.

3.3. *Shippon interior at Sanders, Lettaford, with central drain and tethering post bases along the walls*

Definitions: functions and features

A longhouse can be defined as a house of originally one build where a cross-passage separates animal and domestic accommodation with varying degrees of inter-connection.[1] In plan form the crucial difference between the longhouse and the two or three room cross-passage house is that in the longhouse the shippon (cow-house) and hayloft replace the lower service room and chamber below the cross passage (3.1, 3.8). There are other differences. The shippon end of the longhouse is almost always much longer than the average lower service end, though exceptionally long service ends do occur occasionally. Then there is the downslope orientation of the longhouse: though farmhouses are always carefully sited to gain every possible advantage from the lie of the land, an emphatic down slope site is vital for the longhouse to provide efficient drainage and mucking-out of the shippon. This is further accentuated when the upper end is built deep into the hill side, (sometimes incorporating huge *in situ* granite boulders in the foundations) to give vital weather protection.

In its moorland stronghold the simpler examples of the longhouse perfectly express a unity of form and function as they

3.2. *Higher Uppacott, Poundsgate. View from higher end showing house deeply dug into the hillside*

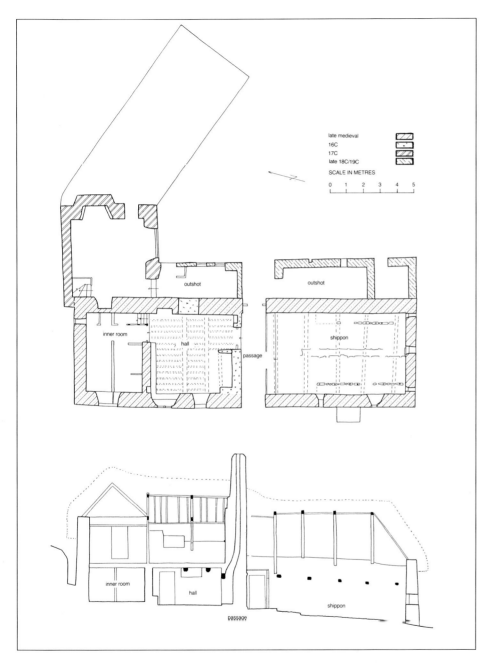

late medieval
16C
17C
late 18C/19C
SCALE IN METRES
0 1 2 3 4 5

outshot

outshot

inner room

hall

passage

shippon

inner room

hall

shippon

passage

3.4. *Higher Uppacott, Poundsgate*
(top) ground-floor plan
(bottom) long section

3.5. Hole, Chagford: (a) front, dung pit in foreground

(b) rear, showing added seventeenth-century wing at upper end

3.6. Oldsbrim, Poundsgate

merge into the landscape to provide human and animal shelter against a hostile upland climate: the walls of Higher Uppacott, Poundsgate (3.2), for example, barely seem to rise above ground level anywhere with thatch sweeping right down to the ground and hardly a window to be seen. This solid simplicity is epitomized by the massive walls of the shippon only pierced by small vertical ventilation slits on the ground floor which keep out the weather, allow air to circulate, and by being splayed internally give a surprising amount of light inside. In the lower end wall of the shippon there is usually a drain exit at ground level with a large square opening above (the dung hole) for mucking-out. These drainage arrangements can be across rather than along the shippon if the lie of the land dictates as at West Chapple, Gidleigh.[2]

The longhouse is classically defined as a house where animal and human access is by the common cross-passage as at Higher Uppacott, Poundsgate, but this arrangement is very rare in Devon. The shippon more often has a door which gives access to the animals independent of the cross-passage, usually but not always with another inter-connecting door from the cross-passage into the shippon. At West Combe, North Bovey, there is an apparently original door in the gable end of the shippon, a rare position (3.7). These separate shippon doors may be original

3.7. West Combe, North Bovey. The door in the gable end of the shippon is rare in this position.

features confirming that there never was shared human and animal access through the cross passage as at Hole, Chagford and Shilstone, Throwleigh (plate 11). In other cases they represent an improvement of the original common access arrangement. West Chapple, Gidleigh, and Pizwell, Postbridge, both have solid cross-walls inserted across the lower side of the cross-passage and shippon doors that are clearly secondary. Above the shippon the hayloft usually required a loading door (again, not at Higher Uppacott). This was also convenient for feeding and some longhouses have slits in the hayloft floor beside the walls allowing fodder to be dropped directly into the mangers below.

Internally the layout of the shippon evolved from the most practical way of sheltering, feeding and cleaning out the cows. This was facilitated by a cobbled floor into which was set a large central drain, the cows usually tethered with their rear ends nearest the drain. Although the upright tethering stakes have usually disappeared (or been replaced by modern equivalents) the drilled stones which held them, as well as granite mangers, are often still visible set into the floor along the walls. The ceiling of the shippon was formed by generally massive and closely spaced cross-beams boarded above, strong enough for the considerable loading that could be necessary when the hayloft was full (Chimsworthy, Bratton Clovelly).

While the shippon end of the longhouse clearly evolved as a cattle shelter, there is some evidence that this function was occasionally eroded by the intrusion of other uses, sometimes

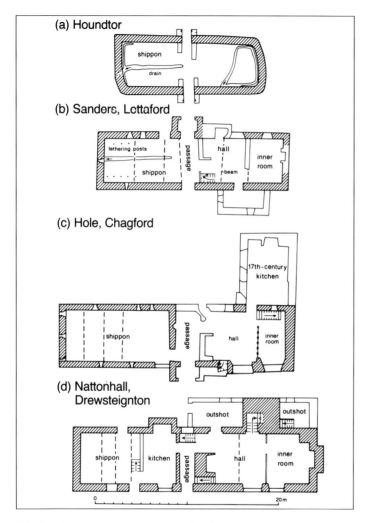

(a) Houndtor

shippon
drain

(b) Sanders, Lettaford

tethering posts

passage

hall

inner room

shippon

t-beam

(c) Hole, Chagford

17th-century kitchen

passage

shippon

hall

inner room

(d) Nattonhall, Drewsteignton

outshot

outshot

shippon

kitchen

passage

hall

inner room

0   20m

3.8. House/shippon separation in Devon longhouses
(a) Houndtor. No partition. thirteenth-century
(b) Sanders, Lettaford. Late medieval house with later external shippon door and relatively modern insubstantial timber partition between lower side of cross-passage and shippon
(c) Hole, Chagford. Original cross-wall separating shippon from house at lower side of cross-passage with inter-connecting internal doors and separate external shippon access
(d) Natonhall, Drewsteignton. Seventeenth-century longhouse with solid cross wall at lower side of cross passage, part of shippon later annexed to house as kitchen

even resulting in the annexing of part of the shippon end for domestic purposes. At Higher Grenofen, Whitchurch, there is evidence that the hayloft was converted to living accommodation in the seventeenth century (there is a staircase of this date on the lower side of the cross-passage).[5] More commonly, extra chamber space was obtained by taking in part of the hayloft nearest the domestic end; at Lower Jurston, Chagford, almost all the hayloft had been converted to provide a total of five chambers on the first floor by the end of the eighteenth century.

As already suggested, at ground-floor level there were varying degrees of separation between the domestic end and the shippon (3.8).[4] At the simplest extreme are houses like Chaddlehanger, Lamerton, and Higher Uppacott, Poundsgate, where there is only a late and insubstantial timber partition between the lower side of the cross-passage and the shippon. At the other extreme are the superior medieval houses like Hole, Chagford, and Shilstone, Throwleigh, where there was always a solid full-height cross-wall separating the shippon from the lower side of the cross-passage with original inter-connecting doors and separate external shippon doors. In between are numerous variations: houses with later timber screens or solid cross-walls inserted to separate house from shippon (Sanders, Lettaford[5]); houses where a section of the shippon nearest to the cross-passage is annexed for domestic use, perhaps as a simple store; and houses that convert part of the shippon to full-blown domestic use, complete with chimney, in the seventeenth century, as in the kitchens formed from the shippons at West Combe, North Bovey, and Nattonhall, Drewsteignton. So the Devon evidence suggests both a considerable range of original late medieval arrangements for separation of the two functions and also much evolutionary development.

Distribution

A distribution map of surviving Devon longhouses shows a striking but very uneven concentration on and around Dartmoor with a thin but significant scatter around the western foothills of Exmoor and a few more scattered examples (3.9). The longhouse of the fifteenth to eighteenth centuries clearly belongs to upland

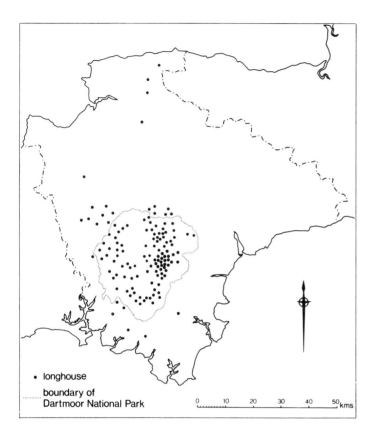

3.9. *Distribution of standing longhouses in Devon*

3.10. *Sanders, Lettaford. Ashlar granite walling to shippon*

Devon and reflects the considerable though often under-rated distinctions between the upland and lowland parts of this vast county. Geologically the uplands are islands of older rock formations, topographically they have most of their land surface above 1000 feet, and climatically they are wetter and colder: central Dartmoor with ninety inches of rain a year is three times as wet as Exeter, for example. These physical differences are historically re-inforced by the evolution of a distinctive agricultural economy, including the availability of grazing rights at certain periods on the open moors, and different tenurial patterns of land holding. Even so, the persistence of the longhouse tradition in these areas is still not fully explained by such factors. Why for example does it not appear in west Devon more

generally where environment and agricultural economy is much more similar to Dartmoor than it is to central or east Devon?

The Dartmoor provenance of the longhouse is accentuated by the apparently ubiquitous use of granite as the building material. It is used as a walling material in coursed or random rubble but is spectacular when worked in huge ashlar blocks, e.g. Hole, Chagford; Sanders, Lettaford; West Combe, North Bovey, and Shilstone, Throwleigh (3.5, 3.7, 3.10, plate 11). Smaller squared blocks are sometimes used to line the inner wall faces. Remnant sections of ashlar are often rendered over during subsequent alterations and additions but are an invaluable guide to the original smartness of the house. Its use in features of display is equally impressive: for chimney stacks, either on the lateral wall with set offs, set backs and even moulded caps, or in ashlar blockwork to the cross-passage with moulded bases and cornices when axially positioned; and for door and window frames.

The longhouse building tradition can provide some of the best external vernacular ornament in stone anywhere in England. While the humble longhouse can mould itself almost imperceptibly into the landscape, the superior examples are clearly designed to show off the prestige of their owners. The front of Shilstone, Throwleigh, for example, with its complete display of medieval to seventeenth-century features – ashlar walling, hollow-moulded windows throughout including king mullions to the hall and parlour, and foliage-enriched spandrels to the cross-passage door – eloquently makes the point that the longhouse could be a house of high social status. Such longhouses are comparable in architectural sophistication and interior comforts and amenities not only with the best contemporary farmhouses anywhere in Devon but also any church or priest's house. (Compare Shilstone with the church house in the centre of its village, Throwleigh,[6] or even the upper hall houses of Neadon, Manaton and Yeo, Chagford.)

Building stones other than granite are used in longhouses away from Dartmoor: the shaly or slatey rubble of Chimsworthy, Bratton Clovelly, or the longhouses around Exmoor. Cob is sometimes used, particularly to heighten walls when re-windowing was undertaken after the flooring-in of an open hall house even in a superior house in a granite area like Shilstone, Throwleigh. There are two longhouses known to be constructed entirely of cob on local rubble plinths at Flood, Drewsteignton and Powlesland, South Tawton.

While the limited distribution of surviving longhouses needs to stressed, it is important to understand that they are not the only house type to be found in these upland areas of Devon. Longhouses are as often located in small hamlets as in isolated farmsteads and these 'longhouse clusters' sometimes contain early houses which are definitely not of the longhouse form. For example, the hamlet of Chapple in Gidleigh parish consists of two former longhouses and a smart two-roomed house without a cross passage from the sixteenth century. At Yeo, Chagford, the hamlet consists of a former longhouse (the present farmhouse), a single-cell sixteenth-century house and a house with a first-floor hall from the late fifteenth to early sixteenth centuries. At Neadon, Manaton, there is no longhouse but a spectacular upper-hall house from the late fifteenth century. Moreover, in the towns and villages of Dartmoor there are other house types, sometimes showing different constructional methods, like the three-roomed cross-passage houses from the late medieval period at Ashburton, Chagford and South Zeal; the church and priest's houses at Throwleigh, South Tawton, Walkhampton and Widecombe; and the partly timber-framed houses of Ford Street, Moretonhampstead, and of Ashburton, which date from the seventeenth century.

A final note of caution about the distribution patterns of longhouses. A distinction has to be drawn between standing longhouses and the question of how widely distributed the longhouse might have once been prior to the fifteenth century: whereas the detailed survey work of recent years has confirmed the restricted distribution of the former, the latter is still an open question. All that can be said for certain at present is that Dartmoor had earlier longhouses, like the excavated examples still visible at the deserted medieval village at Houndtor. But we only know this because a few deserted medieval village sites on Dartmoor have been excavated; we simply do not know whether other early longhouses await excavation in lowland Devon. However, given that these early longhouses are known by excavation in other parts of England, it would not be surprising if future work discovered them either on the relatively rare deserted village sites or on farmstead sites which have been in continuous occupation. Here the excavations on farmstead sites in the area of the Roadford reservoir may prove of particular value because this area is on the western fringe of standing longhouse distribution.[7]

Dating and development

The archaeological evidence suggests a continuity of longhouse building going back at least to the thirteenth century, and we can confidently date the earliest standing example to the later fifteenth century. However, it has already been emphasized that this long line of continuity does not imply that the fifteenth- to eighteenth-century longhouse was a primitive survivor among the evolution of more sophisticated house types. Indeed, the largest of the excavated thirteenth-century houses at Houndtor are over fifty feet long and twenty feet wide, which compares favourably with a typical modern house. It is also usual to distinguish between 'early' longhouses known by excavation (e.g. at Houndtor, Oakhampton Park, Hutholes, Meldon and Beare and North Tawton[8]) and 'improved' longhouses of the later sixteenth and seventeenth centuries, a distinction drawn, for example, by Eric Mercer in *English Vernacular Houses*.[9] But the Devon evidence suggests much less of an evolutionary or even a chronological gap. The Houndtor houses were deserted at some

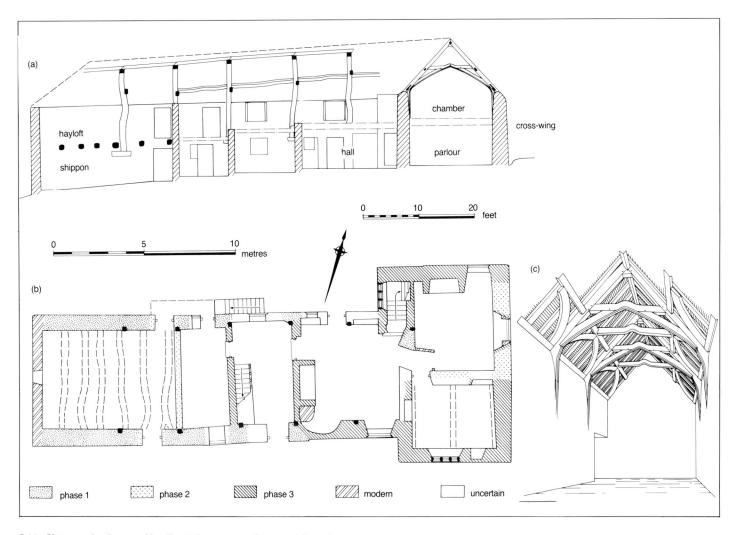

(a)

hayloft

shippon

hall

chamber

parlour

cross-wing

0   10   20
feet

0   5   10
metres

(b)

(c)

phase 1   phase 2   phase 3   modern   uncertain

3.11. *Chimsworthy, Bratton Clovelly: (a) long section, (b) ground floor plan,
(c) reconstruction drawing of former open hall of cross-wing.*

3.12. *Lower Jurston, Chagford*
(right) front view
(below) ground-floor plan

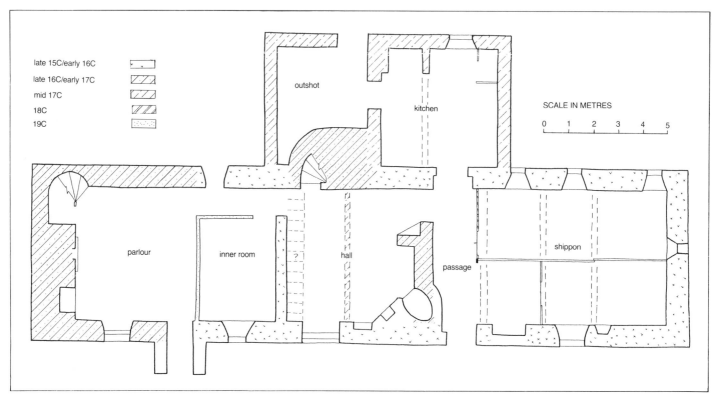

late 15C/early 16C
late 16C/early 17C
mid 17C
18C
19C

outshot

kitchen

SCALE IN METRES

0   1   2   3   4   5

parlour

inner room

hall

passage

shippon

point in the fourteenth century and we can be reasonably sure that some standing longhouses were constructed during the course of the next. Many of them were considerably adapted by the end of the medieval period. At least one example (Chimsworthy, Bratton Clovelly) has two superior medieval building phases (3.11) and another nearby longhouse at Buddle, Broadwoodwidger, has an open-hall extension built on at the upper end of the original hall. And they went on being adapted, extended, partially reconstructed and occasionally newly built at least well into the eighteenth century.

The Devon evidence therefore suggests that longhouses enjoyed a continuity of tradition from the early fifteenth to the late eighteenth century and displayed the same diversity of scale and evolutionary sophistication as is found in all other Devon houses of the period: in the sequence of internal and external development, in high quality medieval carpentry, good decorative detail, and ever more complex plan form reflecting a move towards more specialized room use. Lower Sessland, South Tawton, finishes up with a five room cross-passage-and-shippon ground floor plan, giving the building an astonishing length. Most medieval longhouses show development from open hall to fully two-storeyed house with separate rooms, heated chambers and even garderobes; Sanders, Lettaford, has chambers jettied into the still open hall from both ends, while West Combe, North Bovey, has perhaps the most substantial internal jetty anywhere in Devon. Smoke-blackened thatch survives complete over many a medieval longhouse roof (e.g. Shilstone and Higher Uppacott). While roof carpentry does not perhaps ever quite reach the peak of sophistication of mid Devon, it is still very impressive in its quality, vigour and decoration, with good examples of arch-braced and wind-braced roofs. Jointed, true, raised and hip crucks are all found, with arch-bracing and cambered collars often embellishing at least the central hall truss.

The prestige and continuity of development in size and plan-form of which the longhouse was capable is nowhere better demonstrated than at Chimsworthy, Bratton Clovelly. Its main range has the most massive true and jointed crucks anywhere in Devon, real tree trunks used more or less as they came to hand. Furthermore, the cross-wing is an open hall with cranked collars, arched and wind bracing, and was later converted into two-storied accommodation in the seventeenth century and given a corbelled chimney to heat the first floor. There are several other

examples of similar elaborate development. Shilstone, Throw-leigh, was extended to the rear with an unheated service wing and completely re-windowed with its front re-faced in the seventeenth century to give a unique surviving presentation of conscious and coherent architectural decoration perhaps once more common at that time. Lower Jurston, Chagford (3.12), was enlarged by adding a parlour and chamber to the upper end and had a kitchen built across the rear end of the cross-passage. A similarly added kitchen at Whymington, Sampford Spiney, has a full-height smoking chamber alongside the vast kitchen hearth. At West Chapple, Gidleigh, a smart cross-wing in ashlar blockwork was added in the seventeenth century at the rear to provide a heated parlour and chamber.

Surviving longhouses are very unevenly distributed, with a heavy concentration to the east of the high moor. Within this eastern concentration, most of the grander examples are found towards the northern edge. South Tawton, for example, has superior longhouses and three room cross-passage houses intermixed. To the south examples are more frequent (thirty-eight in Widecombe parish) but more modest. In Widecombe a local fashion was to add a porch wing to the front of the house, elongating the cross-passage and providing an extra service room alongside (Middle Bonehill [plate 8] and Lake). In the humbler longhouse the simple outshot was the only extension (Lower Merripit, Postbridge). Because of the shippon function, all this extra domestic accommodation had to be provided at the upper end, a contrast with the three-room cross-passage house where the lower end could also be developed.

By the end of the seventeenth century the longhouse could boast as much conspicuous quality inside and out as farmhouses anywhere in Devon. Porches could be decorated and have inscribed datestones (3.14); that at Higher Corndon, Wide-combe-in-the-Moor, is even vaguely classical and dated 1718. Inside, the hall ceiling could sometimes be of intersecting beams, the hall walls be decorated with panelling as well as built in benches and even carved bench ends (Cox Tor Far, Peter Tavy), and there are many spectacular stud and panel screens. The one missing element is plaster work, though Nattonhall, Drewsteignton, has some rather primitive seventeenth-century cornices in the grand chambers. This house is a good example of how the longhouse tradition seems to have been able to adapt to new developments as early as the seventeenth century, for it has a

3.13. *Decorated door frames*
(left) Middle Bonehill, Widecombe-in-the-Moor 1682
(right) Corndon Farm, Poundsgate, 1718

spacious hall and parlour, and a wide staircase wing at the rear gives independent access to the lofty chambers; but it is still has an integral shippon.

When did longhouses stop being built? There is an illuminating account in John Swete's diary of 1797 of his visit to Dartmoor when he was taken to a house of a man aged seventy-seven who describes how he had raised this 'small cottage' on a new-take near Blackabrook (plate 13).[10]

I found the interior of the cottage to correspond in every respect with the outward appearance. The door entered into a portion appropriated to the winter reception of cattle belonging to the farm, from thence I passed directly into the kitchen, which was lighted by a sort of window, at the farther end was a large chimney in which blazed a cheerful peat fire, of which fuel as it rose at the indoor they did not seem to be sparing. Near the entrance I observed a ladder which I concluded, must lead to the bed chambers. Up this ran, and found it to be so, in the singular number, for it consisted but one. About twenty feet in length and half that space in breadth, in which as close to each other as those in the long chamber at the College of Eton, there were ranged five beds in which without the interposition of screens or curtaining the old man, his son, and others, amounting to four men and five women every night took their rest. How patriarchal and in the ancient style of doing things.

Conclusions

So the apparently straightforward Devon longhouse is capable of being both originally constructed and subsequently adapted over a wide social and chronological range. The variations, which make every longhouse unique, are precisely why vernacular building traditions are so endlessly fascinating to study, as a basic house type is constantly being re-interpreted to meet ever changing individual requirements. But we are now at the end of this tradition. The author has seen longhouses still in dual occupation with shippons full of cows sheltering against the bitter cold of a Dartmoor winter at Higher Corndon Farm, Widecombe-in-the-Moor, and also seen the shippon being used as a stable, woodshed, implement shed, workshop, hen-house, pigsty, calf rearing house, and lambing shed. But such uses are now a rarity. Hence the policy of the Dartmoor National Park Authority of refusing to allow longhouse shippons to be converted to domestic use if they survive in anything like their original form. There are only a handful left, and unless such an exceptional, but clearly preservationist policy is rigidly applied (with accompanying public financial support for the upkeep of the shippon end), the visible longhouse will have disappeared from Devon by the end of the century.

4.1. *Traditional use of an enclosed yard with cob and thatched buildings in North Devon*

4

Farm Buildings

PETER CHILD

The next few years will probably be the last opportunity to see Devon's traditional farm buildings in anything like their original form. Although the practices for which these buildings were designed have been wholly or partly obsolete for nearly one hundred years, a combination of agricultural conservatism and impoverishment has resulted in their retention into an era for which they have an ever-increasing unsuitability. Intensive mechanization has taken over from intensive labour as the essence of agricultural practice and the buildings required for each purpose are inevitably quite different in character and scale. Obviously there is little incentive to put money into maintaining the older buildings, which consequently must slowly decay. The alternative solution offered to this problem is to turn the buildings to another use; in practice this is virtually always their conversion to houses. A recent tolerance within the planning system for such new residential uses in the countryside stemming from governmental support for farmers to realize their assets in this way, combined with a huge rise in house values, means that the more substantial farm buildings are likely to be converted in this way in the near future. While the best designed of these conversions may retain the overall form of the building, its details and evidence of its working functions will disappear. So on the one hand natural decay, and on the other radical alteration, are likely in the next decade largely to obliterate a heritage of buildings which, although often humble, are almost always both pleasing to the eye and historically interesting.

In 1850 White[1] described the Devonshire tenant as 'at once a dairy farmer, a breeder or feeder of cattle, and pigs, and a grower of corn and cider'. The farm buildings reflected this versatility:

> The buildings are of every variety of character from the antique and dilapidated, to the more modern and convenient ... The better class of farm buildings are generally in the form of a square, close all round, and entered on the south side through a large arched door, under the granary. Immediately opposite is the barn, cider cellar etc., which usually occupy one side of the square, having the corn rick behind. Two sides are for the accommodation of cattle, the back walls being built up to the eaves but the front is in two storeys supported on strong posts and open from the ground to the eaves; the lower storey occupied by cattle; the other kept as a store for their provender ... The fourth side of the square embraces the farm, stable and wagon shed.

4.2. Hand threshing with flails in the early nineteenth century. The labourers are working on an oak threshing-floor with the unthreshed sheaves on one side, the threshed straw on the other. The doors at either end of the threshing floor are open to provide light and ventilation for this exacting work.

This is a description of a somewhat more consistent organization of the buildings than is generally found in the field, but it conveys the essence of the traditional Devon farmyard and it does emphasize the very mixed nature of Devon's farming as late as 1850; the dominance of dairying in the county was a more recent phenomenon, dating from the late nineteenth century, brought about by changing economic circumstances. It is true that some parts of the county (notably south-east Devon) were known as dairying areas as early as the seventeenth century but even here it was far from the exclusive agricultural activity. Much land was 'convertible' i.e. it was not permanent pasture or meadow; Vancouver in 1808 states that seven-eigths of farmland in north

4.3. *An exceptionally large corn barn with two threshing floors faced by wagon doors on either side at Colleton Manor, Chulmleigh. Probably late seventeenth or early eighteenth century*

Devon fell into this category although one-eighth was under corn at any one time.[2] Consequently the balance between the various forms of pastoral and arable agriculture varied according to economic demands or personal preference, but most farms of any substance before 1850 would have been involved in corn (and other crop) growing, raising beef cattle, cider-apple growing, dairying and sheep. All but the last require special buildings displaying both national and local characteristics in their design. The materials from which they were constructed are identical to those of the farmhouses and are described in a separate chapter in this volume.

Barns

The corn barn still dominates the farmyard scene in most holdings, even in the high ground of the moorland fringes. Before the arrival of machinery for threshing the grain out of the heads of corn (which meant that a whole crop could be threshed in one session) it was normal to store the sheaves in the barn (or in a rick yard or 'mowhay' where the barn was too small to hold the whole crop) to be threshed on a demand basis by labourers

4.4. *A South Hams bank barn at Pounds Farm, South Pool. The gable end, typically for this part of Devon, is built into the bank to enable high-level loading in contrast to bank barns elsewhere the rear long wall lies against the bank.*

using hand flails, a slow and laborious method. For this purpose an oak plank threshing floor extended from one long side of the barn to the other, connecting high double doors sometimes of full wall height (4.2). Such an arrangement had multiple purposes: firstly of providing an access and egress for wagons or loaded packhorses (commonly used in the steeper parts of Devon); secondly of providing a light and high area within which to thresh the corn; and thirdly of providing a draught to drive away the dust arising from the threshing and more importantly from the subsequent process of winnowing the threshed corn of dust and chaff by throwing it into the air and catching the grain, using baskets. (For a detailed description of hand threshing and winnowing, see Marshall.[3]) The threshing floor usually divided the barn into equal sections, one normally to be used to contain the unthreshed sheaves, the other the threshed straw. Since the barns had to contain a bulky crop and since also considerable headroom was necessary for the use of flails, corn barns are generally relatively tall and substantially constructed (4.3).

Consequently they tend to survive from an earlier date than other types of farm buildings, with that at the Bishop of Exeter's Palace at Bishops Clyst being the oldest known in the county.[4] This measures 90 ft. long by 24 ft. wide internally and is probably early fourteenth century in date, its large size commensurate with the status of the owner; indeed the emphasis and the size in any holding on corn production can be measured by the size of the barn.

Barns with two pairs of opposed doors are not uncommon; sixteenth- and seventeenth-century barns with jointed-cruck roofs occur and eighteenth- and early nineteenth-century examples are common. As might be expected the walls are of cob or stone (occasionally brick) and the roofs were generally of thatch. The walls are usually plastered internally for the sake of cleanliness and to control vermin.

Jointed-cruck roof trusses are succeeded by A-frames and then king-post or scissor trusses; in the south of Devon there are often no proper purlins or common rafters, simply thick thatching spars.

Openings in the external walls beside the threshing doors are few (sometimes none), limited to loading doors or ventilation slits. The actual doors are commonly sub-divided both for convenience and particularly to create different degrees of draught when winnowing, and have removable central posts to allow access for carts. Usually on either side are a pair of narrow full-height buttresses, sometimes carrying a canopy. These are related to more substantial porches found on barns elsewhere in England, but the Devon examples (except in the South Hams) are generally so slight as to provide little effective shelter and, while, to some extent structural in that they reinforce the sides of the large door opening, are more a traditional feature than a functional one. Sometimes the threshing floor is flanked by beams at eaves level extending from one side of the barn to the other. These perhaps were used to suspend temporary partitions of cloth or leather when threshing or winnowing.

In the South Hams corn barns show marked differences from those in the rest of the county (4.4). Here they are often built end-on into a bank, providing a high level loading door in one gable. They also consistently only have a single divided wagon door placed opposite a simple small door to provide a through draught for winnowing, and these doors may be placed at one end of the barn, not centrally. Large projecting porches flank the wagon

4.5. *A typical small corn barn at Beaford with thatched roof and cob and stone walls. A very shallow porch is formed by buttresses flanking the wagon doors.*

4.6. *A nineteenth-century bank barn at Shop Farm, Broadwoodwidger. The upper floor was used for corn storage and processing and has two doors on the front which served both for winnowing and for pitching down into the yard. The barn is built into the bank so that principal access to this floor is from the rear at ground level where there are two wagon doors. The lower floor was used for housing animals and only has access from the yard in front.*

door and these are deliberately tapered to obtain a better draught; the barns also show a consistent north-west to south-east orientation to use the prevailing south-west winds for the same purpose. The threshing floor is also sometimes placed at one end of the barn instead of centrally.[5]

There are thousands of examples of the corn barn. Sometimes they have been adapted to more modern uses, having floors inserted to function as lofted cow houses or accommodating grain driers. The only major variation on the type is the 'bank barn' (4.6) where sloping ground is utilized to provide two floors, the upper approached from the rear, the lower from the front facing the farmyard. The former was used for corn storage and threshing, the lower generally for animal housing. This was an efficient way of accommodating two functions under one roof. The barn was used in the normal way with a central threshing floor approached by double doors on the bank side which could be faced either with a single loading or winnowing door overlooking the yard, or particularly in the Tiverton-Cullompton area, by another pair of double doors, despite the fact that these could not possibly be used for the through passage of wagons or horses; this seems to be a piece of local conservatism. Cow shippons, stables or wagon houses, or a combination of these, were accommodated in the lower storey. Some bank barns have the sills of the rear loading doors raised two or three feet above two or three feet above the ground, precluding the entrance of a

vehicle but enabling corn to be pitched in at the level of the cart. Such barns started to occur in the late eighteenth century and continued to be constructed throughout the next. They generally are rather better built (usually with stone walls and slate roofs) than are the orthodox barns and are more often to be found on farms owned by estates, reflecting an interest in farm improvement by the large landowners and their greater capital resources. On many smaller farms, the tenants were responsible for the farm buildings and stuck to traditional structures, not being able or willing to do more than renew or repair these.

Horse-engine houses

However, one innovation connected with the barn which was commonly adopted without reluctance by most farmers because of its obvious benefit, was the horse-powered threshing machine and its companion building the horse-engine house, otherwise

4.7. *A threshing machine driven by a horse engine in operation at the end of the nineteenth century. Four horses in the roundhouse provide the motive power for the threshing machine which is being fed with sheaves pitched from a wagon. The grain is being shovelled out from under the machine while the threshed straw is ejected at its further end. The old threshing floor can be seen beyond the machine, while one of the labourers stands on the box where the grain is stored.*

simple wooden posts and with tiled or thatched roofs. Even though the machinery can no longer be seen in engine houses, the massive elm or soft-wood beam which took the upper bearing of the spindle and held the whole device steady usually remains as evidence of the building's former function.

These engine houses are not found nationally; as with bank barns their distribution is primarily in the north and south-west of England. The reason for this is not at all clear but it may be that the relatively small size of Devon farms combined with a mixed agriculture meant that surplus winter labour for hand threshing was not as available as it was elsewhere in England and this justified the expense of installing such machinery. No doubt they were also useful for other permanent machinery such as chaff-cutters, apple crushers and cake- and root-slicers all the year round. They remained in use on some holdings until the 1920s. Some farms such as Teigncombe, Chagford, used water power instead of steam or horse-power to drive machinery via shafts and belts from a water-wheel. Eventually the stationary diesel or petrol engine was to supersede such power sources and threshing is now done as part of a single harvesting operation by a combine.

4.8. *A thatched horse-engine house supported on stone and timber posts at West Chapple, Winkleigh*

known as a round house or horse gin (4.7). These were invented and developed in the north of England at the very end of the eighteenth century and presumably arrived in Devon soon after this. Although the actual machinery has almost everywhere long since disappeared, its existence is evidenced by the buildings created to cover the horses and the driving wheel which supplied the power. These buildings are invariably attached to the barn so that a drive shaft can readily be connected through the wall to the threshing machine housed in the barn. Two to six horses plodded a circular path within the engine house, turning a central spindle by means of long sweeps. The spindle was surmounted by a large crown wheel, which drove a small pinion which turned the shaft through the barn wall to connect to the threshing machine.

The form of the buildings is very varied, semi-circular, polygonal or rectangular in plan, completely open-sided on piers, or with varying numbers and sizes of openings. Stone and slate houses are commonest, but they occur in brick and cob or with

Granaries and rickyards

As long as threshing was done by hand the quantities of threshed and winnowed grain available at any one time was small. Specialist granary buildings of an early date are very rare; compartments for grain storage were provided in other farm buildings, or the grain was kept in the house itself. However, with the advent of mechanized threshing, independent granaries catering for large amounts of grain available from a single machine-threshing appear. Smaller ones are often of timber-framed construction with stone or brick nogging, plastered both externally and internally (the latter to provide clean storage). This exceptional use of timber-framing in rural Devon results probably from the fact that these granaries stand on stone or brick piers or staddles to prevent the access of rats and mice, for which a light framed building is the most suitable design. Timber-framed granaries are commonest in north Devon for no very obvious reasons. More substantial two-storey granaries commonly occur with solid walls, the lower floor being used as a

4.9. *A nineteenth-century timber-framed and thatched granary at Higher House, Atherington with brick piers and nogging*

stable, and the upper for grain storage approached by an outside stair. The interior was divided by boarded partitions into bins for different types of grain. Both types of granary are usually nineteenth-century in date.

Corn was not always stored entirely inside barns, but also outside in ricks in stack yards. The surviving evidence for this is very slight, consisting only of supports for the ricks to hold them above the ground to exclude damp and vermin. Staddle stones, as at Yeo Farm, Chagford, were most commonly used for this purpose, but are likely to have been removed; in the west of Devon (e.g. Combe Park, Broadwoodwidger) stone granite posts were driven into the ground, projecting 2–3 ft to support a framework for the stack. At Bullaton Farm, Hennock, there are two circular rick stands of solid masonry constructed with corbelled ledges to exclude vermin.

Root and manure houses

Root crops for cattle feed became more popular throughout the nineteenth century and root houses may be recognized particularly in improved complexes of this date. These are usually tall buildings with pitching holes as well as doors for their filling with turnips or swedes; they should have direct access to the cattle yards or cow-sheds for ease of feeding. At Lower Jurston, Chagford, the double bank barn has two underground chambers with corbelled stone roofs extending the shippon into the bank; these appear to have been for root storage since there are channels in the top of each at ground level into which the roots could be dropped. Fertilizer stores (or 'manure houses') also occur at this date; these are single-storey sheds with doors large enough to admit a cart.

Cider houses

The other major Devon crop was cider apples. Although cider was made in the Middle Ages, it became a speciality of the county in the seventeenth century and remained a standard part of the agricultural economy until the beginning of this century. While

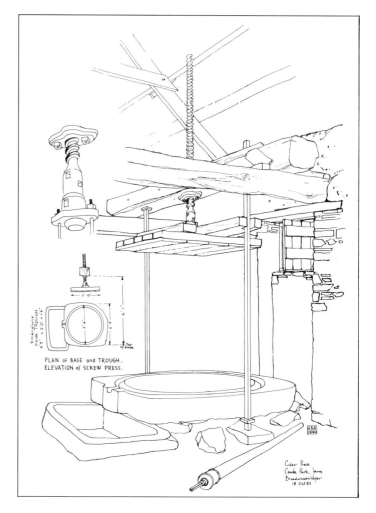

PLAN of BASE and TROUGH.
ELEVATION of SCREW PRESS.

Cider Press
Coombe Park Farm
Broadwoodwidger
18 Oct 85

4.10. *A nineteenth-century cider press from Coombe Park, Broadwoodwidger. Coombe Park now lies under Roadford Reservoir.*

the cider was mostly consumed on the farm (labourers' wages were often partly paid in cider – two quarts a day in the later nineteenth century on the Rolle Estates) or locally, it was also sent elsewhere in England. Daniel Defoe in the 1720s claimed that 10 to 20 thousand hogsheads (perhaps between 650 000 and 1.3 million gallons) were exported to London annually and a 1750 estimate of production in the county was 10 million gallons.

A look at any first edition Ordnance Survey map, particularly of east or central Devon, shows every farm surrounded by its own orchards. Unlike beer, the alternative pre-tea drink, cider keeps well. Moreover it has to be made relatively soon after the apple crop is gathered. Beer, therefore, was made in comparatively small quantities throughout the year and thus remained a domestic activity conducted inside the house. Cider in contrast not only needed substantial barrel storage space for a year's supply, but also a building with a headroom to take the screw press which squeezed the crushed apple to make the juice for fermentation (4.10). Until the nineteenth century the first crushing was done in large circular stone (usually granite) troughs around which a horse pushed a stone crushing wheel connected to a central vertical pinion; sometimes these massive troughs survive complete or in parts lying around the farmstead. They were totally superseded in Devon in the nineteenth century by mechanical crushers consisting of contra-rotating cogged cylinders driven from horse engines. The crushers were usually sited in a loft (also used as an apple store) over the press so that the crushed apple could be fed down to it. The cider house ('pound house') is not a distinctive building externally and is usually only identifiable by surviving machinery. Sometimes it is a building adapted from a different original function, very often a small threshing barn. There is a free-standing early seventeenth-century example at Week, Tawstock, but most are later in date.

4.11. *Linhays still in traditional use at Higher Woolsgrove near Crediton in 1989. These are now being converted to housing.*

Linhays

Livestock buildings on the Devon farm fall into three main categories, the open cattle shed or 'linhay', the closed cattle shed or shippon, and the stable. The first of these only is a distinctive local type; indeed its prevalence in Devon and its virtual absence (apart from a few examples in south Wales and the west Midlands) make it the hall-mark of the Devon farmyard. It had a dual purpose, the sheltering of cattle and the storage of hay. It is characterized by the solid (cob or stone) construction of its rear and side walls combined with a completely open front, the first floor and the roof above being here supported on posts. These posts are mostly of timber rising from ground to eaves, but circular stone pillars sometimes occur, particularly in south Devon, as do granite posts which support the first floor with timber, or even cob, posts above. The roof structure is always a conventional double pitch, the trusses rising directly at the front from the posts (or in the South Hams from a wall plate) to which they are connected by joints of varying complexity. Any of the traditional roofing materials might be used, thatch in the earlier examples, slate or tiles in the nineteenth century. The individual bays of these linhays are not sub-divided internally and although they vary considerably in size are most commonly about 8 ft. wide by 8–10 ft. deep, while the floor of the hayloft (or 'tallet') over is about 6–8 ft. above ground level, with the eaves 4–6 ft. above this. Linhays can be as short as a single bay only or as long as eighteen bays, as at Shobrooke Barton (4.12); commonly they face the principal farmyard within which the cattle ran in winter, sheltering in the lower part of the linhay and with their winter food-stuff readily to hand above. Alternatively, and more conveniently, the linhays are self-contained within their own yard.

4.12. One of the largest linhay ranges in Devon at Shobrooke Barton. Two and a half sides of this nineteenth-century yard contain thirty-six bays of linhays.

Most linhays have subsequently had their fronts partly or wholly boarded over or given doors, and have been partitioned to provide enclosed accommodation but the true type was completely open internally and to the yard. They are not easy to date, but the earliest examples appear to be seventeenth-century, while they were still commonly being constructed until the end of the nineteenth century. Some of the latest examples are 'hybrids' with more orthodox cow houses being given doors and passages serving feeding racks. Some linhays are in positions away from yards where they cannot have been used for housing cattle and it seems that they then acted as cart or implement sheds with a loft over. The overwhelming majority, however, were for the sheltering of cattle for the four winter months. The ubiquity and long life of the form must both indicate that it was an effective design for cattle rearing purposes in terms of the local climate and that such cattle rearing was a continuously important element in the farm economy.

Cow houses

It is much harder to generalize about the fully enclosed cow house or shippon than the linhay. In 1935 it was said that 'on many milk producing farms it is fairly obvious that the original cow shed has been supplemented by the conversion of other buildings. On these farms milking is carried out in as many as three or four different buildings ...'[6] Such alterations brought about by the demands of modern hygiene, new technology and the vast increase in dairying (dairy cows in Devon doubled between 1866 and 1930) resulting from improved communications, have left few traces of old shippons which in any event

*Plate 1. Lime washing in Broadclyst:
pink, cream and white*

Plate 2. Details from two late medieval smoke-blackened roofs: (top) Lower Chilverton, Coldridge, showing wind and arch bracing; (bottom) Middle Clyst William, Plymtree, medieval thatch and smoke louvre in the former open hall

Plate 3. Cob colours: (top left) cream (Doddiscombeleigh), (top right) red (Broadclyst), (bottom left) yellow (Shebbear), (bottom right) light brown (Kenn)

Granite (Chagford)

North Devon shale (Mortehoe)

Slate stone (Kingsbridge)

Chert (Chardstock)

Breccia (Heavitree, Exeter)

Red sandstone (Bishopsteignton)

Plate 4. Examples of building stone used in traditional local building

Hurdwick stone (Tavistock)

Killerton stone (Broadclyst)

Plate 5. South Wood Farm, Cotleigh. A three-room and cross-passage house with axial stack and two-storey porch. The exterior is entirely seventeenth-century but this conceals a medieval core.

Plate 6. Farmsteads dispersed throughout the landscape in east Devon

Plate 7. Collabridge, Dunsford. The three-room and cross-passage plan form of this thatched cob farmhouse can be recognized from the position of the ground-floor windows and the porch. The central stack backs onto the cross-passage.

Plate 8. Middle Bonehill, Widecombe-in-the-Moor: a longhouse with prominent added entrance porch

Plate 9. (left) Corndon, Widecombe-in-the-Moor, showing the shippon end of the longhouse

Plate 10. Granite ash house at Sanduck Farm, Manaton

Plate 11. Higher Shilstone, Throwleigh. The front elevation shows clear evidence of the medieval house in large ashlar granite blocks disrupted by the rewindowing of the house necessary when the open hall was finally floored to create a two-storey building.

Plate 12. 10-11 The Close, Exeter; a
medieval courtyard house designed
for an official of the Cathedral. The
picture shows the entrance arch
leading to the courtyard. Behind is
the two-storeyed hall range.

Plate 13. John Swete's watercolour of a Dartmoor longhouse (1797)

Plate 14. This nineteenth-century watercolour depicts a long gone mid seventeenth-century brick mansion in Exeter. Its off centre front doorway and window arrangement even suggest a similar plan form to 44–46 Magdalen Street, Exeter.

Plate 16. Ornamentation on the façades of two Exeter houses of the mid seventeenth century: (top) sgraffito and carved oak, 225–6 High Street; (bottom) slate hanging on timber-framing, Tudor House, Tudor Street (c. 1660, restored in 1970s)

Plate 15. Two lead rainwater heads (with dates) from the front of 28 Bridgeland Street, Bideford, which include the initials of John and Elizabeth Hooper

Plate 17. The Royal Hotel, Bideford incorporates a house reputedly built in 1688 by the merchant John Davie. It boasts perhaps the finest seventeenth-century interior in Devon, even better than the surviving contemporary gentry houses. The 'Kingsley room' has a magnificent ornamental plaster ceiling and is lined with field panelling. The panel over the fireplace is painted with a landscape scene.

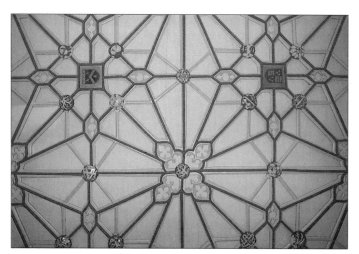

Plate 18. 10 The Close, Exeter

Plate 19. Wall painting, Margells, Branscombe

Plate 21. Painted cupboard head, Pynes, Washford Pyne

Plate 22. Overmantel, Waldronds Cullompton

Plate 20. No. 28 Bridgeland Street, Bideford contains a kitchen dresser built with the original house between 1692-94.

Plate 23. St Mary's Cottage, Newton Poppleford

Plate 24. Painted window reveal, St Nicholas Priory, Exeter

Plate 25. Plaster ceiling, dated 1620, 62 Boutport Street, Barnstaple (left)

Plate 26. Ornamental plasterwork, Clysthayes, Silverton (middle)

Plate 27. Bible cupboard with ornate plaster surround, Wressing Cottage, Kentisbeare (right)

Plate 28. Plaster ceiling, Bellair, Exeter

Plate 29. Interior decoration, Forde House, Newton Abbot

4.13. *A thatched linhay at Deckport, Hatherleigh. The lower floor has largely been enclosed and the original roof supports have been reinforced by telegraph posts.*

were probably never very impressive structures, since cows were traditionally not considered to require much light or air indoors. Probably they resembled the longhouse shippons of Dartmoor with the cows tethered facing the outside walls with a central gutter, all under a hayloft. Bank barns of the early nineteenth century often have shippons on their lower floors with three or more doors facing the farmyard. The cows were tethered in a line facing away from the doors, probably without stalls originally, but later modifications make this a point hard to determine. Stalls subsequently became standard, each containing a pair of cows tethered by a chain attached with a sliding fitting to a post. The passageway behind the cows both allowed them to reach the stalls and acted as a drainage and mucking-out area, the manure being barrowed to a heap in the yard or pitched out directly onto a pile through a pitching hole. Marshall, in 1796, speaks of the linhays being 'used for cows; oxen being generally kept in houses or hovels, provincially "shippens" during the winter'.[7] Oxen were commonly used for ploughing; it has been said that their

standings in the shippon were slightly longer than those for cows.[8] By the mid nineteenth century it was recognized that a lofted building was unsuitable for a cow house mostly because of the excessive heat generated by the cows which could result in pneumonia. Consequently single-storey buildings open to the roof were developed of which the general form in Devon seems to have contained the cattle in a single row facing a feeding passage and a manger. This simple type still survives (although the modern milking parlour now predominates) with concrete or iron stalls replacing the wooden ones and windows inserted to provide adequate ventilation.

Stables

Although oxen were generally used for ploughing and other cultivation work until the middle of the nineteenth century in Devon, horses were used for transport. However, carts were uncommon because of the steepness of the ground and the poor quality of the roads. Packhorses or donkeys and sledges filled this role. 'Hay, corn, straw, fuel, stones, dung, lime etc are all in the ordinary practice of the District [west Devon], still carried on horseback' wrote Marshall in 1796.[9] Stables therefore were to be found in every farmyard but (like shippons) they are sometimes difficult to identify as their relatively simple form and their long disuse and probable conversion leads to their disguise. They are generally lofted, sometimes with accommodation for farm hands above on larger holdings. The presence of windows is often the commonest indication of a stable, since the ventilation provided by these was not considered necessary for cattle. The stable ceiling was higher too than that of the cow house, while stalls, where they survive, are more substantial slatted wooden structures reflecting the horses' kicking power. Horses were usually stalled singly; each stall would have a hay rack as well as a manger. Mid nineteenth-century stables characteristically have a central door with a window on either side and a loading door for a loft or granary above; outside steps to the latter are common. Loose-boxes as well as stalls are found in larger stables while sometimes there is a separate stable for the farmer's trap or riding-horse ('nag'); this may be adjacent to a trap-house.

4.15. *A nineteenth-century stable at Great Trill near Axminster, with grain storage above the horse accommodation*

4.16. *Pigsties at Knowle, Crediton. These are sophisticated for Devon in that they have feeding doors but, as is common, they have no open run for the pig.*

Cart sheds and ash houses

Structures not associated directly with animals in the farmyard commonly include cartsheds, open-fronted on posts, often of three bays and traditionally facing north away from the sun. These can be single-storey lean-to structures or of two storeys, the upper often being a granary. They are almost all nineteenth-century in date since carts were rare before then. In Bridford parish there were no carts at all in 1800 but fifty by 1850.[12]

A rare building (most commonly found around Dartmoor) is the ash house where the ash from the house fires was stored for later spreading on the fields (plate 10). These are generally circular (about 12 feet high by 12 feet in external diameter) with a conical roof and a hole at ground level for shovelling up the ash.[13] In east Devon it was mixed with turnip seed so as to spread the latter more sparingly.[14]

Pigsties, hen houses, dovecotes and bee-boles

Farm buildings for other animals besides horses are not common. Sheep were not permanently housed, while pigsties of the usual form with a little run only occur in later complexes the traditional Devon sty being no more than a shed. Marshall observed this in 1796 and said that pigs often went to pasture with the cows in west Devon;[10] no doubt they shared the farmyard and linhays with them too. He also observed that the hens 'roost in the cool open air';[11] certainly chicken houses of any age are not obvious although there is a nineteenth-century example with stone nesting boxes at Welltown, Walkhampton. Some free-standing dovecotes have been recorded. These are perhaps more to be associated with genteel living than agriculture as such, although many farmhouses and barns have a few nesting holes in one wall. Less common are the curved niches for the straw skips which preceded the modern beehive ('bee-boles') which may also be found in house or garden walls.

Farmstead layout and evolution

The vast majority of buildings described above congregated around the farmhouse; isolated barn and cattle shelters are relatively rare, although in the South Hams there is a fairly regular occurrence of substantial corn barns standing alone in the fields. (The reason for this regional variation is not obvious). Independent cattle linhays are also a feature of the reclaimed pastures of the Braunton Marshes.[15] Within the farmyard the buildings do not occupy a set pattern but generally make up a courtyard form, with one, two or even three sides consisting of linhays (4.17, 4.18), allowing the cattle from these to stand out in the yard and to water in a central pond; sometimes there are double yards. Manure from the animals houses was taken to a dung heap in the yard; sometimes this was a specially constructed pit, as at Hole, Chagford (3.5). The farmhouse itself usually forms part of one side of the yard but can stand free of it entirely. Although farm buildings can sometimes be attached to the farmhouse this appears never to have been the original plan; the house was conceived as a separate entity, except in the case of longhouses (see Chapter 3). Not all farmsteads take a courtyard form; there are some linear layouts (Combe Park, Broadwood-widger) and some quite random ones.

4.17. *The farm complex at Shobrooke Barton. Linhay ranges form the east and south sides of the yard and part of the west side. The rest of the west side is occupied by stables and the east side by a pair of corn barns with a horse-engine house attached to their rear. The angled building at the entrance to the yard is a granary.*

4.18. *Whelmstone Barton, Colebrooke, from the south. The building which forms the north side of the yard is a substantial sixteenth-century corn barn enlarged in the eighteenth century. Linhays make up the other two sides, with a cider house forming the end section of the south range. A separate cart shed stands on the west side of the seventeenth-century farmhouse.*

Nineteenth-century farm improvement

As agricultural practices were examined scientifically and rationally from the late eighteenth century onwards, the mutual relationship of the farm buildings became a subject of much thought, particularly to take advantage of the introduction of new machinery and agricultural techniques. Most Devon farms were too small to be much affected by the new thinking but on the larger estates some total rebuilding took place, if not on the scale of the larger farms of east and central England. An early example is reported in Vancouver at Haldon.[16] This has many interesting features combining both traditional and innovative ideas of the period. There are no enclosed cow houses for instance, although the two-storey linhay is replaced by single-storey open-fronted cow and ox houses. The horse-engine is conveniently and unusually located on the ground floor of a bank barn. A very large area of building is devoted to cider-making and cider cellars; on the other hand there is an un-Devonian emphasis on pig-rearing with elaborate sty ranges. A simple single courtyard form is still retained and despite the advocacy of multi-yard arrangements by nineteenth-century improvers, this remained the normal practice in Devon even when substantial rebuilding took place as, for instance, on the estates of Lord Clinton in south-east Devon in the later part of the century. Many of the farms here were re-built under the supervision of Mark Rolle, primarily in order to attract new tenants in a time of agricultural depression.

At South Farm, near Otterton, an entirely new yard was constructed at the rear of the existing farmhouse which was extended. The only other buildings which were kept were the pound house and cellar (the above-ground cider store) to which were added a new pound house and cellar, the old pound house being converted to another cellar, to make three in all, illustrating the important role of cider in the Devon agricultural economy. The re-building of the rest of the complex was around a simple yard, measuring internally 95 ft by 105 ft. The house and its garden faced south into this yard, and opposite to them was a cow house for sixteen cows under a corn barn, flanked by a root house and a straw barn in either corner. The west range connected to the root house consisted of calf and fattening houses, while the east range contained a further cow house and stables. All the cattle buildings had rear feeding passages linked to either the straw house or the root house and a round house at

4.19. *Mr Pearce of Monkokehampton at the wagon entrance to his corn barn.*
One of the studded doors is divided in two horizontally in the traditional
manner.

the rear of the south range provided motive power for agricultural machinery needed in the processing of straw or other fodder. In this respect the layout is efficient and convenient, but the placing of the corn barn over the cow house seems quite the opposite since the sheaves would have had to have been lifted up to first floor level before they could be stored or processed. The barn even includes a threshing floor at this first-floor level with steps to the yard on one side and a drop at the other. In a separate block outside the yard and facing a road are two implement sheds, one with granary over, and a manure house for fertilizer storage, another sign of changing agricultural practises. A large piggery with twelve sties flanking a small open yard abuts the side of the farmhouse close to the back kitchen. Much emphasis is put on drainage, with a complete system to collect rainwater and liquid manure and sweepings into separate tanks (to prevent the latter being diluted by the former). The buildings at South Farm fortunately remain largely intact today as a witness to the agricultural practices of a Devon landed estate in the nineteenth century and to the quality of craftmanship and design a landowner considered reasonable even for a relatively small tenanted farm.

This chapter is not based on any systematic study of farm buildings, only on personal observation and on the very limited published works on the subject. There is a desperate need for a concentrated study of this part of our architectural heritage as, unlike the farmhouses themselves, the farm buildings are either going to disappear completely or be so altered as to be virtually unusable as historical artifacts. Moreover we are just within touch of the era of traditional farming and there is, therefore, a human resource of memory and experience which can still be tapped.

Both the buildings and their owners have been taken for granted as permanent features of the country scene; shortly this will be no longer so. Although the interpretation of farm buildings set out here will, it is hoped, hold generally true, in the absence of systematic study there are many glaringly obvious gaps in this description. For instance, regional differences between one part of this very large county and the rest have hardly been touched upon; the distinctive nature of the barns in the South Hams shows how much variation there may be. Many questions need to be answered. The size of farm buildings varies considerably, those in the west and north of the county appearing much less substantial than those in the south and east. Is this simply a factor of poorer land, or is it due to different farming practices, or to the smaller size of the holdings, or possibly to different systems of tenure? Is the type of farm layout consistent throughout the county? Are the various buildings in a consistent relationship or is this random? And is their orientation regular or haphazard?

The date of construction of buildings is another great problem as most of them offer little detailing on which to hang a date, and for instance, the nineteenth-century re-roofing of an older barn is common. However, there certainly is variation in constructional detail (particularly in the linhays) and it may be possible to build up a collection of datable examples to act as a source of reference for this purpose. Unfortunately, Devonshire farmers were not generally in the habit of inscribing dates on their new buildings and documentary material is very poor. Nevertheless there is a large amount of evidence to be culled from such readily available sources as the tithe maps and early Ordnance Survey editions, even if earlier estate maps and records are uncommon. The material is there to be gathered and the rewards would be great, but the task is a substantial one.

5

Town Houses up to 1660

MICHAEL LAITHWAITE

The houses of the more important Devon towns of this period contrast sharply with those of the countryside. Whereas medieval farmhouses abound, town houses of the same date are rare. Exeter still has some good examples, but these are mostly of two or three storeys. Houses originally of only one storey, or with an open hall, are confined almost entirely to the smaller towns of predominantly 'rural' character, such as Bovey Tracey. Ashburton is the most 'urban' town to retain houses with roof-trusses blackened by the smoke of an open hearth, and even here the surviving examples are in rural-style houses. Instead, Devon towns contain some of the finest urban domestic architecture of the late sixteenth and seventeenth centuries in England, the result, apparently, of a widespread rebuilding stimulated by the prosperity of the early post-medieval cloth trade, together with the more specialized involvement of some towns in activities such as the tin trade and the Newfoundland fisheries.

Losses by fire have, however, distorted the picture considerably, especially among the smaller towns. Bradninch, Crediton, Honiton, Ottery St Mary and Tiverton suffered heavy destruction in a series of fires ranging from the end of the sixteenth century to the middle of the nineteenth. Of the east Devon towns, only Cullompton retains more than the odd house of pre-eighteenth-century date, and even there a fire of 1839 destroyed about a hundred houses. The use of thatch for roofing probably accounts for the great extent of these disasters. Tiverton, which reputedly lost over 400 houses in the fire of 1598 and 600 in that of 1612, did not

5.1. *Totnes. View down the High Street, showing the Butterwalk. Nearly all the houses are sixteenth- and seventeenth-century, refronted in the eighteenth and nineteenth centuries.*

ban thatch until another 298 houses had been burnt down in the fire of 1731. In the rest of the county, town fires seem to have been less common and there is no record of the major towns being seriously affected. Nevertheless most of Chudleigh was destroyed in 1807; Great Torrington suffered from fires in 1601 and 1724, and most of North Tawton was said to have been burnt down in the first half of the nineteenth century. Despite this, some early houses remain in the centres of both towns. The most obvious reason for the difference between east Devon and the rest of the county is that roofing-slate was more readily available in the west. Its early use in the general run of domestic buildings is difficult to prove, but it is clear that a well-organized slate industry existed in south Devon by the twelfth century, when slates were being transported to south-east England for use on important buildings. By the 1530s the Dartmouth church-wardens' accounts show that the town was regularly slating its small houses, and by the middle of the sixteenth century its port books record a regular export trade of slates (or 'shindelstones') to the Continent.

Raiding parties from French ships caused damage to some port towns, although the instances of this are surprisingly few, considering how often England and France have been at war. Teignmouth, however, was burnt in 1340 and 1690, and part of Plymouth was destroyed in 1403, as was Dartmouth (according to the French, but not the English) in 1404.

Many of the towns that escaped destruction through fire were largely rebuilt in the late eighteenth and early nineteenth centuries. It was not only the seaside towns that were affected in this way, but some of the more important inland ones as well, notably Kingsbridge and Tavistock. In 1796, in Kingsbridge, 'a spirit of improvement pervading the inhabitants', as one contemporary writer put it, a major programme of rebuilding was undertaken. Today earlier buildings in the town are limited almost entirely to the courtyards behind the street-frontages.

In more recent times redevelopment has been less kind to the towns, although late Victorian rebuilding of the type that transformed towns in the more industrial parts of England had relatively little effect here. The most serious losses have occurred since 1940, especially in the leading towns of Exeter, Plymouth and Barnstaple. The first two of these suffered badly from bombing in 1940–3, but indiscriminate demolition in all three towns has removed a veritable treasury of buildings since the war.

They still contain some of the most important pre-eighteenth-century town houses in the county, but constant vigilance is needed to protect them against redevelopment schemes.

Much of the best urban domestic building of the sixteenth and seventeenth centuries, and occasionally earlier, is to be found in the smaller towns, notably Dartmouth and Totnes, whose houses are unexpectedly grand in relation to the size of the towns. Ashburton and Topsham are also good towns with houses lower on the architectural scale, and besides these there are the 'rural' towns with high-quality houses, such as Bovey Tracey, Hatherleigh and Moretonhampstead.

It needs to be stressed, however, that early urban architecture is often hidden behind altered façades and roof-lines. Some of the most interesting houses discussed in this essay were identified only as they were about to be demolished. They must be taken as typical of many that have yet to be discovered.

Urban building materials

Building materials differed markedly between the town and the country. Whereas cob and stone were the almost invariable walling materials in the countryside, at least externally, the towns were characterized by the use of timber-framing, slate-hanging and brick. Cob was used much less often, and its use tended to diminish as the architectural character of the town became more 'urban'. Barnstaple is unusual in retaining boundary walls and back-street cottages of cob in the town centre, while Totnes has only two cob buildings, and they are on the very edge of the town.

Stone, of course, was commonly used, but the lack of easily workable stone in most parts of the county means that there are few façades comparable to those in the oolitic and liassic limestone areas of Dorset and Somerset. As a result, the better building stones were often brought considerable distances to provide dressings for the grander town houses. To take Totnes as an example once again, Beer stone from the south-eastern extremity of Devon, granite from Dartmoor, and red sandstone from Torbay were all used to supplement the unyielding local slatestone. The Great House of St George at Tiverton has one of the best stone façades among the town houses (5.2). One of the most decorative is on a house in the Square at North Tawton,

5.2. *The Great House of St George, Tiverton (1631). One of the best early seventeenth-century examples of a grand town house, with its broad street façade in stone.*

5.3. *No. 16 High Street, Totnes (1585). A rare example of Classical design in a sixteenth-century English town, built for a merchant, Nicholas Ball, in the year of his mayoralty. It was probably gabled originally.*

which has an early sixteenth-century bay window of stone with eight round-arched lights separated from each other by moulded shafts. The most remarkable, despite some nineteenth-century alterations, is at 16 High Street, Totnes, an exceptionally rare example of late sixteenth-century classical design in a period when most English townsmen were content with houses of essentially medieval appearance (5.3). It has delicately carved friezes (probably of Beer stone, beneath the paintwork) at first and second-floor levels, Doric and Ionic pilasters flanking the second and third storeys, and a loggia in the ground storey. The friezes bear the date 1585 and the initials 'N.B.' (for Nicholas Ball, a wealthy merchant).

Timber-framing is found in most of the towns where pre-eighteenth-century houses survive, even in Moretonhampstead on the edge of Dartmoor. Its presence is the more remarkable in that Devon has very little rural timber-framing and most of that is confined to entrance porches (see pp.14–15; 1.2). In towns it was rarely used to build a whole house, but for 'mixed construction,' that is to say for one or two external walls in an otherwise stone or (in two cases) brick-built structure (5.5). In such buildings the front wall is invariably timber-framed, and usually the back one as well. The former is commonly 'jettied', the framing of each storey being projected a foot or so beyond the line of the one below. The side-walls of stone are carried forward so that they are visible from the street, and are corbelled out at each storey to match the jetties. The back walls are rarely jettied, and there are some cases (mostly mid-seventeenth-century or after) in which the front is also unjettied, the floor-levels being marked (and the rain thrown off) by cornices or small pent-roofs (5.8). Where a house is built on a corner, both street-frontages are sometimes timber-framed and jettied, as at 16 Edmund Street, Exeter, now moved to the foot of West Street (5.4). The reason for this urban use of timber-framing, and of mixed construction in particular, is still a matter for debate. There are similar town houses in areas where stone, rather than timber, was the traditional building material throughout the length of England, from Cornwall to Westmorland. In Norfolk there was a parallel tradition of mixed brick and timber construction. Probably the need to make a dramatic architectural effect in the confined spaces of a town had much to do with it. Timber may have been a relatively cheap medium for elaborate carving and, of course, it permitted devices like jetties and overhanging gables.

5.4. *The House that Moved', Exeter. Transported to the foot of West Street on rollers in 1961. A late medieval corner house with both street-fronts timber-framed and jettied; original shop windows (with later infilling) in ground storey.*

5.5. *Two examples of mixed-construction town houses: 70 Fore Street, Totnes (left) and 33 St Andrew's Street, Plymouth (right). The late sixteenth or early seventeenth-century timber-framed fronts are jettied out between side-walls of stone.*

5.6. *Nos 52 (left) and 54 Fore Street, Totnes in the mid nineteenth century. Jettied, gabled houses, respectively of 1692 and 1607. The patterned framing at No. 54 is now plastered over. (Drawing by N. W. Deckament in Devon Record Office).*

5.7. *Carved oriel window in the Butterwalk, Dartmouth (1635–40)*

The framing in Devon is usually concealed by eighteenth- or nineteenth-century plaster or slate-hanging, but where it is exposed to view (or where it has been examined during building work) it seems to derive equally from the traditions of the west Midlands and south-east England. A common type consists of a series of close-set uprights ('close-studding'), sometimes divided by horizontal timbers (a 'middle rail') halfway up each storey. In some medieval examples (mostly in Exeter) a downward curved ('tension') brace is halved across the uprights. Carved medieval timbering is rarely seen; the best (probably as late as the mid

sixteenth century) is at 46 High Street, Exeter, the front of which, in addition to being jettied, has deep coving beneath the second- and third-storey windows. The third storey has an enriched bressumer surmounted by moulded shafts, and at one end is a carved wooden figure. Post-medieval houses provide several examples of decorative woodwork, especially in the brackets and framing of oriel windows; the Butterwalk at Dartmouth is one of the best (5.7). A favourite device, dating mainly from the early and mid seventeenth century, is to arrange the wall-framing in small rectangular panels and put a light moulding or a chamfer on the edges of the timbers; Totnes has two fronts in this style and there are several in Dartmouth. The post-medieval patterned framing characteristic of the west Midlands is no longer to be seen in Devon, but it was used, both in Barnstaple and Totnes; a nineteenth-century drawing of 54 Fore Street, Totnes (5.6), shows quatrefoils and 'star' pattern in a gable dated 1607. The ground storeys have usually been altered to insert modern shop-fronts, but New Street, Plymouth, retains a fine series of carved wooden doorways, two of them (Nos 37 and 38) adjoining what appear to be early seventeenth-century shop windows.

5.8. *Tudor House, Exeter. Built c. 1660, this house is the best surviving example of early slate-hanging, here using very small shaped slates. Note the continuous pent-roofs between the floors.*

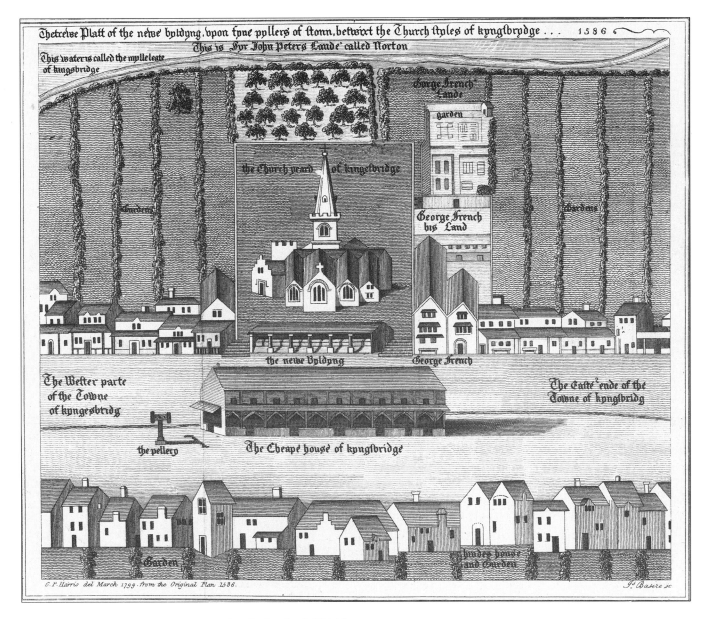

The treue Platt of the newe byldyng, vpon fyue ppllers of ftonn, betwixt the Church ftyles of kynglbrydge . . . 1586

This is Syr John Peters Lande called Norton

This water is called the mylle leate of kingsbridge

George French Lande

garden

the Church yeard of kingeſbridge

George French his Land

Gardens

Gardens

the newe Byldyng

George French

The Weſter parte of the Towne of kyngesbridg

The Eaſte ende of the Towne of kynglbridg

the pellery

The Cheape house of kynglbridge

Garden

bradeg house and Garden

G. P. Harris del March 1799 from the Original Plan 1586.

Js Basire sc

5.9. *A late eighteenth-century copy of a plan of Kingsbridge, dated 1586. The burgage plots, which run back to the mill leat, have directly influenced the house forms.*

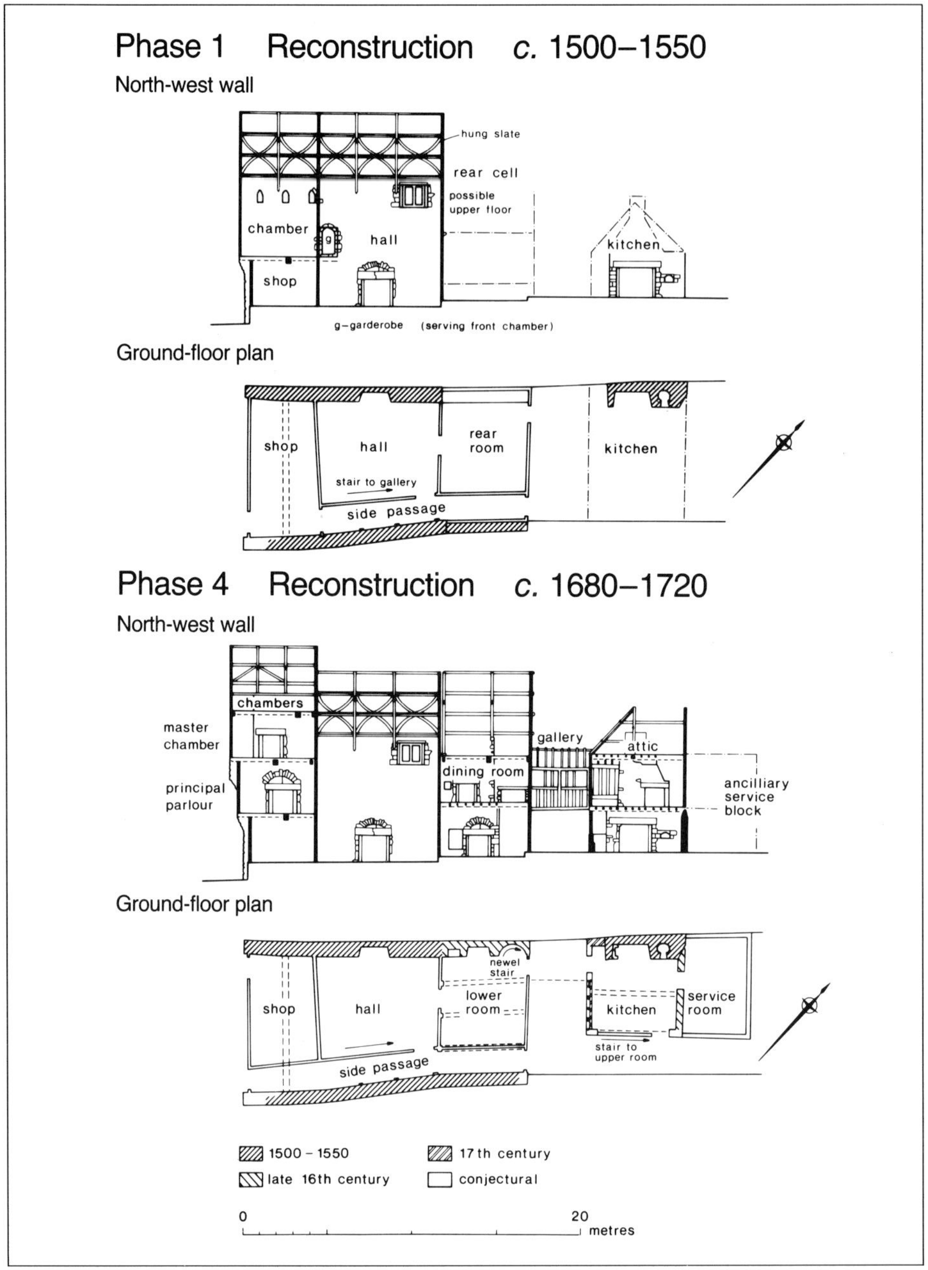

Phase 1   Reconstruction   *c.* 1500–1550

North-west wall

hung slate
rear cell
possible upper floor
chamber
hall
kitchen
shop
g–garderobe   (serving front chamber)

Ground-floor plan

shop   hall   rear room   kitchen
stair to gallery
side passage

Phase 4   Reconstruction   *c.* 1680–1720

North-west wall

chambers
master chamber
gallery   attic
dining room
principal parlour
ancilliary service block

Ground-floor plan

newel stair
shop   hall   lower room   kitchen   service room
stair to upper room
side passage

1500 – 1550   17th century
late 16th century   conjectural

0   20
                     metres

5.10. *38 North Street, Exeter, Drawings showing two phases of its development; reconstructed by Exeter Museums Archaeological Field Unit from evidence uncovered during demolition in 1972.*

By the middle of the seventeenth century exposed framing seems to have been going out of fashion, and was being replaced by much less elegant (but often equally well constructed) timbering designed to be concealed from the first. Whether the 'cladding' was originally intended to be plaster or slate-hanging is now virtually impossible to tell. Certainly no external plasterwork with datable early features now survives, apart from that filling the panels between the timbers at 225–226 High Street, Exeter; these have a design of raised strapwork dating perhaps from about 1660. The earliest surviving slate-hanging, datable by documentary evidence to the same period is at the Tudor House, Exeter (5.8). The tiny shaped slates used in this façade are otherwise found only in a small patch in a gable of 1 and 3 Wolborough Street, Newton Abbot (which bears, for no obvious reason, the date AD 1690 in modern lettering). There is, however, a possibility that slate-hanging was in use in Exeter by the sixteenth century, for a single slate was found nailed to the original rear gable of 38 North Street, at a point where it had been converted into an internal wall by the addition of a further room in the later sixteenth or early seventeenth century.

Brickwork was occasionally used instead of stone in towns in conjunction with timber-framing, as at the Tudor House, Exeter, and at 74 High Street, Barnstaple. Nearby, at 98 High Street, it almost certainly formed the original 'nogging' or infill for the early seventeenth-century timber-framed front of the back block (demolished in 1981). Fronts wholly of brick do not seem to have come in until the mid seventeenth century (see p. 27). Exeter had an all-brick mansion dated 1659 (44–46 Magdalen Street, demolished in 1977), and in Paris Street there was once a brick façade similar to the type known in south east England as 'Artisan Mannerism' (plate 14). Documentary references show that the chimneys of some small houses in Dartmouth were being built of brick as early as the 1520s and 1530s, while Barnstaple has a good series of diagonally-set brick chimneys starting with 8 Cross Street in 1635. The Barnstaple bricks of this period were probably made locally, although 12 000 are known to have been shipped in from London in 1617. Exeter was receiving cargoes of London brick by 1579; it may have been manufactured in Holland, which was sending brick direct to Exeter by 1612 and to Dartmouth by 1618.

House plans

The plans of town houses were governed to a great extent by the cramped sites on which they were built. It was not so much that land was scarce in towns as that their inhabitants, no doubt for commercial reasons, placed high value on having a frontage on one of the main streets. The result was the characteristic 'burgage' plot, deep and narrow-fronted, sometimes as much as 400 ft long and as little as 9 ft wide, fully built up along the street but with a long garden behind. A 'bird's-eye' view of Kingsbridge, drawn in 1586 (5.9), shows just such a lay-out.[1] By the seventeenth century, cottages were beginning to be built on these gardens, until, by the late nineteenth century, the whole plot was often built up from end to end, both with dwellings and with minor industrial buildings. Excavations, such as those in the area adjoining the medieval Exe Bridge at Exeter, have shown that parts of some towns were already built up in this way during the Middle Ages.

The most constricted house sites, however, had no back gardens at all, which was a serious deficiency in a period when few houses had inside privies and domestic refuse was usually buried in the householder's own ground. At Totnes such houses were built on narrow strips of land in front of the churchyard and the meat market, and even on the edge of the infilled ditch at the foot of the castle mound. Quite wealthy citizens were willing to endure these conditions for the sake of a good frontage, as 11 High Street, Totnes, testifies: a grand three-storeyed house with interior plasterwork dated 1586, backing directly on to the churchyard.

A wide range of house-plans resulted from these constricted sites, as builders tried to provide adequate daylight for long narrow houses closely overlooked by their neighbours. No classification is wholly satisfactory, but the plans are most easily considered in two main categories: those built at right-angles to the street and with their gable-ends facing it, and those built lengthways along the street-frontage with their roofs usually (but not invariably) parallel to it.

Gable-end plans

In Devon the 'gable-end' houses are by far the more interesting group, and their tall, narrow façades, commonly three or even four storeys in height and up to 25 ft in width, remain a dramatic feature of the townscape, especially in Exeter and Totnes. Probably only Chester can now provide a comparable range of English examples. The essential feature of this plan was that it was only one room wide, but anything up to three rooms deep, all the rooms being of equal width. Independent access to the ground-floor rooms was often provided by placing a side-passage between the front and back doors. The grandest of these houses were 36 and 38 North Street, Exeter, both demolished within the last twenty years (5.10). They were of late-medieval date (probably of the early sixteenth century, since they had original fireplaces in the hall) and when first built consisted of a two-storeyed section at the front with a lofty open hall of equal height behind. Beyond that in turn was a third section, also two-storeyed, although at No. 38 the upper room was a post-medieval heightening of an originally single-storeyed or low two-storeyed structure. A two-storeyed kitchen block lay a little further down the plot, separated from the main house by a small courtyard, and at first-floor level at No. 38 (and formerly at No. 36) a gallery linked the two blocks. At No. 38, which was thoroughly examined by the Exeter Museums Archaeological Field Unit before demolition in 1972, the kitchen block was medieval, although heightened and much altered in the late seventeenth century, while the gallery was an addition of the late sixteenth or earlier seventeenth century (5.13).

Houses like these are occasionally found elsewhere in England, notably at Chester, Southampton and Taunton, but they are exceedingly rare, and no other examples have been found in Devon. Assuming that others did exist, one reason for their disappearance may have been the problem of lighting the central hall. Its windows had to be placed in the side-walls, and were only practicable if the adjoining houses were either shallow enough or low enough to avoid blocking them. Significantly, the hall windows at 38 North Street were set high up in the side-walls. With the general enlarging of houses in the early post-medieval period, and, still worse, the general insertion of upper floors into open halls, the problem must have become insuperable. Houses of this sort could, however, be remodelled relatively easily by demolishing all or part of the timber-framed front, back and internal partition-walls, in order to rebuild within the shell of the stone side-walls. In this way a house could be reduced in depth, as seems to have been done at 198 High Street, Exeter, where, during demolition in 1975, medieval paintings were found on the wall of the former courtyard behind the front block.

The nearest late sixteenth- or early seventeenth-century equivalents to the two Exeter houses seem to be 44 High Street and 70 Fore Street, Totnes, although in this case no parallels yet appear to have been found elsewhere in England. No. 44 was heavily altered in the eighteenth century, but No.70 is very well preserved and has been restored for use as the Totnes Museum (5.5, 5.11). Here the plan consists of two rooms, front and back, with a passage to one side of the ground floor. Between the rooms, in place of the medieval hall, is a stair compartment, the winding newel stair of which allows space for a small landing at each floor and, on the upper floors, a closet. Quite exceptionally there is an external side passage,[2] but it was not used as a source of light. Instead, the outer wall of the stair compartment was recessed to create a small light-well. Behind the house is a spacious courtyard, having at the rear a second block, formerly (as doorways at first-floor level show) linked to the first by a gallery. At the junction of the gallery and the back block there was clear evidence of a former staircase, a most unusual feature and far more characteristic of French gallery-and-back-block houses. Both staircase and gallery were rebuilt in about 1970 on roughly the lines of the original.

Much more characteristic of the gable-end houses are those only two rooms deep, without either an open hall or (originally) a stair compartment in the centre. The best and most numerous examples are in Totnes, but there are several in Barnstaple (notably The Three Tuns, High Street[3]), Dartmouth and Exeter, and at least one in Topsham (74 Fore Street). Apart from 46 High Street, Exeter, all appear to be post-medieval. No. 54 Fore Street, Totnes, is typical, having a three-storeyed front block linked by a first-floor gallery to a two-storeyed rear block. Taller rear blocks seem to have been uncommon. However, 18 North Street, Exeter, evidently had one of three storeys, since galleries survive at both first and second-floor levels, themselves a unique feature in gable-end houses. Four-storeyed front blocks are almost as unusual; 41–42 High Street, Exeter (dated 1564), are of this height, and so was 227 High Street, Exeter, of which only the ornate façade now survives.

The staircases in these houses (where evidence remains) were originally unlit newels tucked into the corner of one of the rooms, against the side-wall farthest from the entrance. The position of the original stair is usually identifiable only by a semi-circular recess in the wall, the plan almost invariably having been modified in the eighteenth or nineteenth century to insert a framed open-well or dog-leg staircase between the front and back rooms. At Totnes the earliest framed staircase in this position, at 52 Fore Street, is dated 1692. No doubt the introduction of skylights provided the incentive for the change in design, since carved balustrades are only worthwhile if they can be properly seen. At 74 Fore Street, Topsham, a late seventeenth- or early eighteenth-century framed staircase has been crammed into a turret at the end of its gallery adjoining the front block, but this seems to be a unique arrangement.

As in the larger houses, the side-passage is a common feature, but it tends to be omitted where the frontage is particularly narrow. The fireplaces, like those in nearly all the gable-end houses, are set in the side-wall farthest from the entrance, but there are odd examples of a stack placed between the front and back rooms, as in 69 High Street, Totnes, and 182 Cowick Street, Exeter (demolished in 1959).

Some idea of the use to which the rooms were put can be obtained by relating information from wills and probate inventories to surviving houses. Although much material was lost through the bombing of Exeter Probate Registry in 1942, a group of sixteenth- and seventeenth-century inventories survives among the records of the Exeter Court of Orphans, and comparisons can be made with inventories from other parts of England, especially Chester. The ground-floor front room usually seems to have been a shop, and this was apparently unheated, for when the structure can be examined thoroughly, it rarely proves to have had an original fireplace. Behind it lay the hall, or dining-room, and beyond that again, in the back block, the kitchen. In some houses the back block was two rooms deep, with a parlour or dining-room at the front and a kitchen behind. Manor Cottage, behind 68 Fore Street, Totnes, is the best example, its front room formerly having had a moulded plaster ceiling. At 98 High Street, Barnstaple, the ceiling remains, although most of the rest of the back block has been demolished. On the first floor of the front block the front room often seems to have combined the functions of parlour and bedroom, sometimes being known in Exeter and

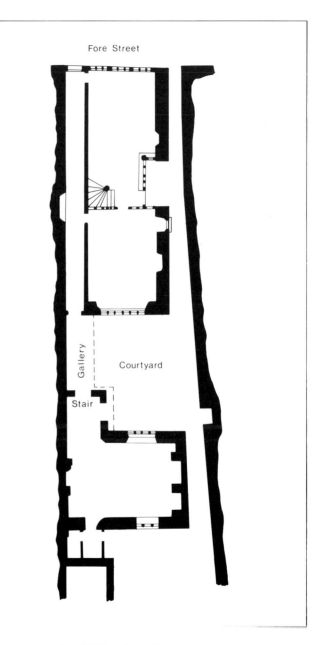

5.11. *Ground-floor plan of 70 Fore Street, Totnes*

Totnes as the fore hall. The rest of the upstairs accommodation was given over mostly to sleeping, the master of the house usually occupying the chamber over the hall. Occasionally there seems to have been a study or counting-chamber at this level.

The smallest type of gable-end house has only one room on each floor, although the rooms can be of considerable height and floor-area, and even the medieval examples can contain as many as three storeys. Documentary evidence from other counties suggests that the ground floor was often a shop, with the hall on the first floor and the bedroom on the second floor. Some of the Exeter houses (notably the one opposite the foot of Stepcote Hill, the 'House that Moved') support this interpretation, but at 13 Higher Street, Dartmouth (The Cherub, a late medieval house) the ground floor has an early fireplace, and this probably indicates that it was used as a living-room. A two-storeyed example, 49 Wolborough Street, Newton Abbot, perhaps of the mid sixteenth century, was later extended at the back. It had early fireplaces on both floors (5.12). Like many of its type it has a narrow frontage and was designed without a side-passage. By contrast, 55 High Street, Totnes, is three storeys high and 20 ft wide and did have a passage, since the seventeenth-century ovolo-moulded stud-and-panel partition with the main ground-floor room remains in position. This house (altered in the early eighteenth century) probably had a detached back block originally, as did an early sixteenth-century house of similar type, 14 High Street, Totnes (remodelled as part of Barclays Bank in 1968).

Galleries and back blocks

Houses with galleries and back blocks deserve special comment, for they are virtually unknown in other counties.[+] In Devon examples are widely distributed; they include houses built side-on to the street as well as with gable-ends. They are known to have existed in Barnstaple, Dartmouth, Exeter, Plymouth, Tavistock, Tiverton, Topsham and Totnes. The best parallels for these houses are on the Continent, especially in France, where galleries, sometimes elaborately carved, already existed in the late Middle Ages. In Devon, by contrast, they all seem to be post-medieval, a fact which suggests the fashion may have originated in France. Significantly, perhaps, there are numerous examples

in Rouen, which was one of the ports most visited by Devon merchants in the sixteenth and seventeenth centuries. Detached back blocks did exist in Devon towns in the late Middle Ages, however, and it could be that a French fashion was grafted onto an existing English tradition. Coronet Place, Kingsbridge, and 14 High Street, Totnes, both had late-medieval detached back blocks, as did a house found by excavation at Joy Street, Barnstaple. At 38 North Street, Exeter, the medieval house and back block were linked together by a gallery (5.13) in the late sixteenth or early seventeenth century.

Few of the existing galleries have sixteenth or seventeenth century details on the surface, and some can be proved to be additions of the eighteenth or nineteenth century. However, the gallery at 38 North Street, Exeter, probably typical of many others, originally had mullioned windows from end to end, and in its lower part chamfered stud-and-panel walling. The gallery at 52 Fore Street, Totnes, (dated 1692), retains a complete range of mullioned windows, now concealed by external boarding. Less typical, perhaps, were the open galleries at 128 Boutport Street, Barnstaple, and 47 High Street, Exeter, the latter having a railing of late seventeenth- or early eighteenth-century balusters.

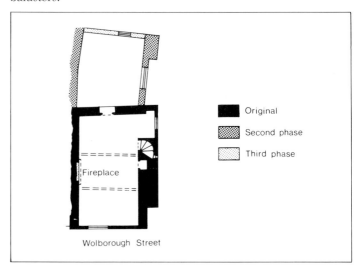

5.12. First-floor plan of 49 Wolborough Street, Newton Abbot. A gabled mid sixteenth-century house with chimney and stair-turret projecting on right-hand side. Two rooms deep, the rear room a later addition.

5.13. *Gallery at 38 North Street, Exeter, during its demolition in 1972. It originally had mullioned windows from end to end, but some mullions had been removed to insert larger sashes or casements in the eighteenth and nineteenth centuries.*

5.14. *No. 32 New Street, Plymouth, restored for use as a museum c. 1929. Probably a mid seventeenth-century remodelling of an earlier house. One room wide with dormer-gable over the centre of the façade.*

Side-on plans

Houses built side-on to the street vary enormously in layout according to the width of their plots. Most are only one room deep, further accommodation being provided by a rear wing set at right-angles to the frontage to form an L-shaped plan. In the wider fronted examples the plan was sometimes extended to contain two rear wings and a rear range, thus creating a full courtyard plan. Alternatively, detached back blocks were used and two of these could produce a house of considerable size. A small group of examples from the sixteenth and seventeenth centuries are two rooms deep; these, too, occasionally have detached back blocks. One common feature is a gabled roof-line, either a series of short roofs set at right-angles to the street or a row of dormer gables creating the same visual effect.

The smallest of these houses are only one room wide with a side-passage, the rear rooms slightly narrower than the front range and lit by a courtyard along one side. Such plans are better known outside Devon, notably at King's Lynn, Oxford and Tewkesbury. In Devon the earliest of them is at 39 High Street, Barnstaple. Its front range was rebuilt in the eighteenth century but the rear wing (perhaps an open hall originally) has medieval cruck roof-trusses. No. 33 St Andrew's Street, Plymouth (5.5), is a classic sixteenth-century example, recently restored as a museum, with only a stair compartment and one large room on each floor of the wing. Its jettied, timber-framed façade is remarkably well preserved, retaining its original doorway and, on the upper floors, its oriel windows, the whole finished with a twin-gabled roof (this last, however, being a restoration of the 1920s). Also at Plymouth, 32 New Street (which is open to the public) is a more modest version of the same plan, being only two-and-a-half storeys high with a dormer-gable over the centre of the façade (5.14). It appears to be a seventeenth-century enlargement and remodelling of an earlier house, and gives a deceptive impression of spaciousness at the back, due to the plot having been widened at this point at the expense of its neighbour.

A very grand, but much more altered version of the plan can be seen at 62 Boutport Street, Barnstaple. This looks like any Regency house from the front, and the whole structure of the first floor has been removed, giving the ground-floor rooms an unnatural loftiness. Its seventeenth-century first-floor plan can be reconstructed from the dimensions of the three moulded plaster ceilings (plate 25). (They are among the finest in Devon, and serve to represent the county's great tradition of urban plasterwork, which seems to have been strongest in Barnstaple and Totnes: see Chapter 7.) The plan apparently consisted of one room at the front and two in the wing, the latter separated by a chimney-stack which now displays a fireplace only in the rearmost room at ground-floor level. The front room of the wing has a great barrel-vaulted ceiling (dated 1620), and must surely have been the chamber over the hall. The smaller rear room, however, has what appears to be a false hammerbeam roof discernible under the plaster-work, perhaps the remnant of a medieval open hall. The ceiling of 1620 bears the arms of the Company of Merchants of Spain, indicating, presumably, that the occupant of the house was a merchant engaged in the trade with Spain.

Devon towns seem to have few striking examples of houses of the two-rooms-and-cross-passage plan, although these are common in other parts of the country. The best to have been studied in detail so far is 33 North Street, Ashburton (demolished in 1970). It was a simple medieval house, originally of only one storey, to which had been added a two-storeyed rear wing with a wall of jettied timber-framing towards the courtyard and a corbelled fireplace and garderobe on the first floor. A still smaller sixteenth-century house of the same plan was 15 and 17 Highweek Street, Newton Abbot (demolished in 1975), which had an internal frontage-width of only 23 ft. It probably had an upper floor from the first, the hall being heated by a fireplace in the rear wall. The building was fully understood only after archaeological excavations in 1976 and 1980, which revealed the foundations of a matching house next door, under No.13, and provided some evidence to suggest that the smaller ground-floor room was used as a shop.

A much grander mid sixteenth-century variant of the type is 43 High Street, Totnes (now a Costume Museum). It was fully two-storeyed and with a rear wing from the start, the latter considerably enlarged in the late sixteenth and early seventeenth centuries. The front range had only a single room (probably a shop) on the ground floor, together with a side-passage leading into the narrow courtyard at the back. Behind the shop is the former hall with a newel staircase in one corner and an imposing granite chimneypiece in the rear wall. Beyond that is a third room of some quality and then the former kitchen. Two good rooms occupy the front of the first floor with a single room (heated by a

5.15. *Manor House, Cullompton (1603). A house of rural plan-type, but with an ornate multi-gabled, timber-framed front characteristic of urban building.*

mid sixteenth-century fireplace) above the hall.

The so-called Manor House at Cullompton (in fact thought to have been the house of Thomas Trock, a merchant) has the full three rooms and a cross-passage along the street frontage and a short kitchen wing disguised under a much larger eighteenth-century extension at the rear. Dated 1603, the main range has three jettied storeys and a series of short roofs set gable-end on (5.15). Another early seventeenth-century house of this type (formerly dated 1631), the Great House of St George in St Peter Street, Tiverton, develops the rear wing a stage further, with a series of small rooms before the former kitchen is reached at the far end. A passage provides direct access to the kitchen without passing through the intervening rooms (an advanced feature for this date), and there was originally a staircase leading off it, of which only the turret now remains. Externally the house is less dramatic than the one at Cullompton, for it is built wholly of stone and the roof of its main range lies parallel to the street, but it does have a dormer-gable at either end.

The best medieval example of a full courtyard plan is Nos 10 and 11 The Close, Exeter, now occupied by the Bishop of Crediton. This started as a simple range along the frontage, but was later enlarged so that the hall range now lies at the rear of the courtyard (5.16, plate 12). The earliest surviving purpose-built courtyard house seems to be the Prysten House in Finewell Street, Plymouth (open to the public), apparently designed in the late fifteenth century as a private house, despite its traditional ecclesiastical associations (5.17). Built round three sides of a courtyard abutting another building, it is oddly lacking in main rooms of any size and had galleries facing the courtyard in the manner of an inn.

The courtyard tradition survived unusually late in Devon, since 28 Bridgeland Street, Bideford, still used the plan in 1692–3, although in other respects it was an up-to-date house of its period. In Barnstaple, 25 Castle Street is an earlier seventeenth-century example (although much altered) with ranges round three sides of a courtyard. Nos 73–74 High Street, Bideford, which has a fine early seventeenth-century ceiling in its front range, may be the remnant of a similar house.

It seems that it was mainly the larger side-on houses that had detached back blocks; however, a one-room-wide example of the seventeenth century exists at 128 Boutport Street, Barnstaple (the North Country Inn). The front block, only one room deep, was remodelled in the early eighteenth century; behind it, however, is a tiny courtyard (now covered in) with original galleries on both sides leading to a two-rooms-deep back block. A slightly larger version of the same plan existed at 4 Vauxhall Street, Plymouth, before demolition in 1963.

The other surviving houses with detached back blocks have also been partly rebuilt, although what remains is still impressive. Coronet Place, Kingsbridge, its front block rebuilt in the late eighteenth century, has two late-medieval back blocks; the first was clearly domestic in function with a pointed-arched doorway, the second a storeroom or stable. 'Little Priory', at the rear of 65 Fore Street, Totnes, appears to have been the back block of a similar house. One end has now been demolished, but it still retains a late medieval roof and an imposing granite chimney-piece of about 1600, with flanking columns and a corbelled hood. The front block appears to have been rebuilt as two houses in the late sixteenth or early seventeenth century; the western house, now 65 Fore Street, being in the same occupation as the back block. Even grander was 7 The Close, Exeter, now converted into

5.16. *Ground-floor plan of 10 The Close, Exeter. No. 11, next door, used to be part of No. 10.*

the Devon and Exeter Institution. It had two domestic back blocks, the first containing the hall and the second the kitchen. Alongside the kitchen was a parlour, which still survives, with moulded plasterwork, wooden panelling and carved overmantel.

A probate inventory of 1630 listing the goods of John West of Tiverton, clothier and merchant, gives an impression of the internal arrangement of a house that must have been of similar type.[5] It apparently had only one back block, but both that and the front block were of three storeys, linked together by galleries at all three levels. The street range seems to have contained the shop, hall and buttery, with a separate dining chamber, buttery and bedroom on the floor above. The dining chamber, however, contained a bed as well as three tables and ten stools, while the chamber over the shop had a table and seven stools besides two beds. The position of the kitchen is not specified, but by implication it must have been in the back block, along with the 'pastery'.

The most interesting of the two-rooms-deep houses is 8 Cross Street, Barnstaple (1635). It is only one room wide, but considerably broader than other such houses with two spans of roofing at right-angles to the street. The rear part has at one side a dog-leg staircase with turned balusters, a forerunner of the arrangement common in terraced houses of the eighteenth and nineteenth centuries. At the rear is a back block, now joined to the main house and reduced to a single storey; a first-floor gallery was demolished in 1987. A late medieval version of the same plan is 35–37 High Street, Totnes, except that it is two rooms wide and has never had a gallery; the position of the original staircase is unknown. Three-gabled houses of this type are rarely found in the county. The Rose of Torridge on Bideford quay is a much-altered early seventeenth-century example, one of its gables having been destroyed by fire. The interior has been somewhat remodelled, but it was probably three rooms wide originally. There is unlikely to have been a back block, since the building lies at the end of a shallow plot fronting on to the medieval Allhalland Street.

Two-rooms-deep houses were also created by adding a second range on to the front or back of an existing building. Such developments usually seem to date from the late seventeenth century or after, but at the time of writing a sixteenth-century example had been newly identified at 3–4 Market Street, Tavistock. Although it had been divided into two separate houses, perhaps as early as the second half of the seventeenth century, evidence remained of a high-quality house with moulded ceiling-beams and a wall painting, the added front range slightly shorter than the one behind.

Terraced houses and houses built in pairs

Devon has no examples of the fine late medieval terraced houses to be found in places like Cerne Abbas (Dorset) and Tewkesbury. The best is the row of two- and three-roomed medieval cob houses at 8–12 Fore Street, Silverton, wholly rural in other respects with chimneys projecting from the front walls. Silverton is now only a large village, but it once had a market and a fair. Other terraces probably wait to be discovered in the larger towns, although from previous experience they are likely to be recognized only after close archaeological investigation. Just such a case was 15 Preston Street, Exeter (demolished in the 1970s), a

much-altered isolated building which proved to have been originally part of a row of at least three timber-framed houses.

Paired houses are commoner, no doubt because they were often of higher architectural quality, probably replacing a larger house on the same site. Nos 41–42 High Street, Exeter (dated 1564) are a good pair of gable-ended examples (5.18), while 48 and 50 Fore Street, Totnes, are quite grand, with moulded plaster ceilings on both first and second floors. Surprisingly humble examples of the type were 13–17 Highweek Street, Newton Abbot, already discussed; they had mirrored plans, the shops or service-rooms adjoining each other in the middle and the halls lying at the outer ends.

Butterwalks

The last, but by no means least, important feature of Devon town houses is the group of arcaded walks: rows of houses built out

5.17. *The Prysten House, Finewell Street, Plymouth. A courtyard house believed to have been built by Thomas Yogge, merchant, at the end of the fifteenth century.*

5.18. *Nos. 41–42 High Street, Exeter (1564). A pair of gable-ended houses built as one structure*

over the pavement on columns. The surviving examples are the Poultry Walk and Butterwalk at Totnes (5.1), the Butterwalk at Dartmouth, and the unnamed and rather fragmented walk at Plympton St Maurice (5.19). No other county has as many, and the Totnes Butterwalk is remarkable in having one house (35 High Street) with late medieval stone columns. Among English towns, only Chester, Ludlow and Winchester have arcaded walks of as early a date. Not all the Totnes examples are medieval, however, or even replacements of medieval originals, for there is a reference of 1532 to an arcade being added to an existing house. What is plain is their association with the markets, since deeds of both 1532 and 1611 refer to stalls being rented out beneath them. The Dartmouth example is a much later development, built on land not reclaimed from the sea until the sixteenth century and bearing the dates 1635 and 1640. Little is known about the Plympton houses, which are thought to be of the late sixteenth or seventeenth century. Their presence in a planted medieval borough is interesting, none the less, in view of the theory that associates these arcaded walks with early medieval town planning, and in particular with the 'bastides' of south-western France.

It is possible that the existing examples are merely the survivors of a feature that was once common in Devon towns. Strip-elevations of Crediton, drawn before the town was destroyed by fire in the eighteenth century, show extensive arcades on both sides of the main street.[6] They include some quite grand houses of the

5.19. *Plympton St Maurice. Arcaded houses in Fore Street: a modest version of the butterwalks at Dartmouth and Totnes*

fifteenth to seventeenth centuries, but also some in which the arcade is merely a single-storeyed pentice, or canopy, attached to the front of the building. Similar structures are shown on the 1586 view of Kingsbridge and it may be that they represent an early stage in the development of the arcades.

6.1. *The Customs House, Exeter Quay, built 1680–81*

6

Town houses of the late seventeenth and early eighteenth centuries

JOHN THORP

The mercantile activity which paid for the fine timber-fronted town houses described in the previous chapter soon revived after the Civil War. Indeed documentary evidence from Exeter, for instance, shows that towns enjoyed far greater prosperity in the following hundred years, peaking around 1700.[1] Reasons for this included the collapse of the monopolies of the London merchant guilds in the 1670s and 1680s which cleared the way for the Exeter master fullers to export their finished woollen serge cloths direct to the Low Countries.[2] At the same time Dartmouth mariners plied a lucrative trade with Newfoundland and the small north Devon port of Bideford profited from trade with the North American colonies which included the import of that luxury commodity, tobacco. The picture is not all expansion. Totnes, for instance, was not as important as it was earlier, but its decline was relative; it was still a rich town.

This period of prosperity for Devon coincided with an interesting and experimental period in terms of domestic architecture as the merchant and lower gentry class abandoned the local vernacular architecture of favour of national styles. Many of these people were well educated and well travelled. They also had access to an increasing number of printed pattern books which disseminated fashionable designs throughout the country. They wanted, and more important, could afford the latest styles in their houses. Sophisticated visitors to the county in the late seventeenth and early eighteenth centuries like Ceilia Fiennes and Daniel Defoe were impressed by the technology they saw, the society they met, and the range of goods available in the town shops.

The new style

Despite the influence of the Renaissance on Elizabethan and Jacobean England the appearance of the merchants' houses along the main streets of Devon towns continued the medieval style; oak-framed fronts between stone party walls with jettied upper floors and gabled roofs. Through the first half of the seventeenth century the houses grew larger and their fronts were

6.2. *No. 17 Cathedral Yard, Exeter: a late-seventeenth-century house with original windows above first floor level. The plastered timber-framed front has no decoration.*

increasingly ornamented reaching an apogee shortly after 1650 and exemplified by the magnificent double-fronted 225–6 High Street, Exeter (plate 16). Here the front of the main rooms on the first and second floors display a riot of moulded and carved oak and even the panels between the timbers are enriched with strapwork patterns of *sgraffito* plasterwork. Next door to this High Street house and built a little later in the century is No. 227 with its impressive façade. In some respects it is traditional: oak-framed, it jetties out from floor to floor, and is surmounted by a gable. In other ways it is different. Here the decoration is minimal and concentrated on the arrangements of the fenestration; the windows are taller, their mullions and transoms are flat-faced with very shallow mouldings and the whole effect is more severe, more in the spirit of classically-inspired Renaissance architecture.

Elsewhere in Exeter there are other houses from the second half of the seventeenth century which are built in traditional style but devoid of external decoration. Their timber-framed fronts are clad with plaster. The double-fronted 67 South Street (next to the White Hart Hotel) is a reasonably easy example to recognize but others are more difficult. Over the Well House, No. 17 Cathedral Yard, Exeter (6.2), is gabled but has no jettied upper floors or any exposed timber-framing. Similar houses with plain plastered fronts occur in most Devon towns, many of them unnoticed. Often their gables have been removed and their windows replaced. Some contemporary town houses around Dartmoor are attractively slate-hung. A good group of these can be seen in Ashburton. (For more details of slate-hanging see pp. 23–4 in Chapter 1.)

However, all these houses represent the old vernacular tradition. A new style of architecture had arrived in Devon and perhaps the best example of it is Exeter Customs House built in 1680 on Exeter Quay (6.1). As the export trade burgeoned after the Restoration, the Exeter City Council embarked on an ambitious and expensive scheme designed to facilitate the export and import traffic. The Exeter Lighter Canal to Topsham was refurbished and the quay was transformed with new warehouses, a transhipment shed and the splendid Customs House itself. Most of these buildings still remain as an impressive monument to a city which was then the third provincial port in England. This Customs House was built with a warehouse wing adjoining to its left but was otherwise completely symmetrical. Originally the main centre part broke forward from the end bays over an open arcade. The arcade has been filled in and the right end bay brought forward flush with the main front. Also the front windows have been replaced with sash windows but original mullion-and-transom windows remain at the back (6.3).

In the new style the roof is either hipped or parallel with the front and the eaves are often provided with a cornice. Nevertheless, old-fashioned front gables continue right through this period. The new-style window openings are usually uniform and regularly spaced. The windows themselves are taller than before. They usually contain timber mullion-and-transom frames which are flat-faced. Most commonly they contain rectangular panes of leaded glass with iron casements. The sash window was in use by the later seventeenth century but does not seem to have been widely adopted until well into the following century. Common features of the contemporary brick buildings are segmental arches over the windows and flat bands of brick projecting at the floor levels.

The use of brick as a building material represents another break with the past; until now it had not been a traditional building material in Devon. Brick grew in popularity throughout England in the sixteenth and seventeenth centuries and by the eighteenth was the preferred walling material throughout the kingdom, although it did not penetrate the more remote areas until the era of railway transport. London, the increasingly influential focus of politics and cultural power, had set the tone for the nation. Here, where good building stone was unavailable, the great Tudor palaces were built of locally-produced brick and in the seventeenth century brick buildings steadily took over in the capital, partly due to a series of building regulations which outlawed external timber framing, but more due to the popularity of Flemish and Dutch styles of architecture. In Devon, brick is very rare before c. 1650 although the Exeter Port Books show that bricks were imported from the 1470s through to 1752 but in greatest volume from c. 1660–1710.[3]

Apart from one or two rural gentry houses the earliest bricks in Devon are all found in or near the ports and are imported 'Dutch' bricks. At first these were reserved for show, such as the lining of the fireplaces inside and external chimney shafts, for example the first floor fireplaces (the principal parlours) of Nos 10 and 12 Duke Street in the Dartmouth Butterwalk built in 1635, and, just round the corner, 4 The Quay, Dartmouth, (dated 1664) with its

6.3. *Original windows at rear of Exeter Customs House. Notice the barred and shuttered lower windows on the bonded warehouses (left).*

fine 'Dutch' brick star-shaped chimney shaft. From Exeter there is archaeological and documentary evidence for a sizeable local brick industry in the town by 1650[4] and from then on brick slowly takes over as the preferred building material in Devon towns. However it must be stressed that many town houses continued to be built of stone and timber-framing clad with plaster. In Totnes, for instance, brick houses are rare before the late nineteenth century.[5]

New concepts in house plan

Such changes in the external appearance of houses in the second half of the seventeenth century were accompanied by internal changes, more obviously involving the arrangements and layout of the rooms. In the long term these interior improvements were to prove the more significant.

In the hundred years or so before the Civil War Devon town houses had altered hardly at all in their layout. The previous chapter describes their form in detail. In terms of privacy and convenience these houses had inherent disadvantages. Firstly some rooms were inter-connecting. For instance, it was sometimes necessary to go through the rear room of the main

6.5. *An exceptionally fine ornamental plasterwork door head from 28 South Street, Great Torrington (dated 1702).*

6.4. *Pinbrook House, Pinhoe, just outside Exeter, was built in 1679 by John Elwill, one of the most successful Exeter merchants. It has a symmetrical front and an experimental plan form in which the central cross passage leads to corridors off each side to corridors along the back of the house to projecting stair turrets each rear end.*

house to gain gallery access to the back block. Secondly, rooms could be awkwardly located in relation to each other as at 41 High Street, Exeter (dated 1564), where the first-floor front room was evidently used as a dining-room (the fireplace includes a warming oven) but was far from the rear-block kitchen. Thirdly, in only a few cases was it possible to light the staircase naturally. Despite these problems similar houses continued to be built through the eighteenth century but from *c.* 1650 onwards houses with new features and different layouts were also being constructed.

One general improvement was the upgrading of the main staircase. Most sixteenth and early seventeenth century houses had winding newel staircases. Examples still survive, at 33 St Andrews Street, Plymouth and in the houses of the Dartmouth Butterwalk. After *c.* 1650 new houses were built with comparatively grand framed staircases with turned oak balusters.

The narrow town centre properties allowed little scope for variation of plan form. The traditional house type was simply developed in the second half of the seventeenth century as the framed staircase, off the side passage, became the main division between the front and back rooms. Similar houses appear in London as early as 1658 and in King Street, Bristol, by 1664.

Another house of this date, 4 The Quay, Dartmouth, is the earliest dated example in Devon (although the corner site meant there was no need for a passage here); and 67 South Street, Exeter, a two-room wide variant of the same plan, must date from the 1660s or 1670s. However, most Devon examples are from later in the century, for example 144 Fore Street, Exeter, and 52 Fore Street, Totnes, (1692). At Topsham 27–29 Fore Street, (dated 1693), comprise an interesting terrace of three small contemporary brick houses with the same central staircase plan. These were not shops; here each ground floor front room was a heated parlour or dining room and the rear room a kitchen. At the same time many older houses were brought up to date by replacing their newel stairs with larger framed staircases, for example 18 North Street, Exeter and 65 Fore Street, Totnes.

The more experimental houses were built in the expanding outskirts of the prosperous towns like Exeter, Topsham and Bideford. There was a very good group just outside the old South Gate of Exeter but sadly most were demolished in the 1970s. Nevertheless some were recorded by Exeter City Council's Archaeological Field Unit ahead of demolition and deserve mention here. Although the later seventeenth-century tax returns suggest that the parish was one of the poorest in the city some very fine houses were built in the second half of the century.[2]

Nos 44–46 Magdalen Street had been made by refronting and converting a fine three-storey brick mansion built by one John Matthew in 1659. It had an L-plan with the main block built along the street containing the principal rooms; a parlour one end, dining-room the other with a kitchen wing to rear, and an entrance hall with a cross-passage through the building alongside. Behind the entrance hall was a large stair block in the angle of the two wings. This must be considered as an early example of a 'modern' house because it attempts to synthesize the new concepts of plan and design inspired by the Renaissance. Here the front door was linked directly, if a little awkwardly, to the grand staircase through both the passage and entrance hall. Thus the staircase centralizes the circulation around the house on all floors and most of the rooms were provided with independent access from the stair landings. Also the layout of the rooms was rationalized, most obviously placing the kitchen adjacent to the dining room. Furthermore the clear site allowed all the rooms and the stairs to be well lit and pleasantly proportioned. The one Renaissance ideal the house failed to achieve was a symmetrical

6.6. No. 8 Cathedral Close, Exeter built c. 1690, is one of the earliest double-depth rear-staircase-plan houses in Devon. The façade was modernized in Georgian times but the arrangement of windows is original.

front. The entrance hall and passage arrangement pushed the front doorway right of centre.

Holloway House, Holloway Street, Exeter (demolished in 1980) was a late seventeenth-century brick mansion built only a few hundred metres from John Matthew's house (plate 14). It had a very similar L-plan but included a significant improvement. Here the staircase was brought into the entrance hall and although there were opposing front and back doorways there was no passage partition here. The stairs rose along, that is to say parallel with, the rear wall and therefore the entrance hall was wide, with doorways to one side. Consequently the front doorway was still not central.

These new houses were one room deep, which was wasteful in the use of space and also expensive in materials. A double-depth house was a much more efficient and compact structure and also better suited to an urban situation. There is a late seventeenth-century house with a double-depth plan still standing between the sites of John Matthew's house and Holloway House: Bishop Pasterfield House, Bull Meadow Road. This house was once larger but the original core remains. Its plan is made up of front and back rooms either side of a central entrance hall with a rear staircase. The principal rooms were those at the front with kitchen and services to rear. Here the entrance hall is central and relatively narrow because the framed staircase rises against, that is to say at right angles to, the rear wall. Another similar house from Exeter is 8 The Close (behind the Law Library) which was first recorded as being leased in 1690 (6.6). In Torrington, 28 South Street is dated 1702 and is a particularly well-preserved example of the new double-depth house type (6.5).

This house type represents the first fully-realized 'modern' house. The rear staircase plan allows the stair to be well lit and it is directly linked to the front doorway; indeed it is a showpiece feature to be seen as soon as the house is entered. Also it enables an elegant façade to be designed, symmetrically arranged about the central front doorway. As Frank Kelsall pointed out in his study of London houses of the late seventeenth century,[6] this rear staircase plan was to become the national norm in the Georgian and Victorian periods; it was ideal for the terraces of speculative builders of the eighteenth and nineteenth centuries. The plan form could be reduced in width to provide the usual Georgian terrace house; one room wide with side-passage to the rear staircase.

Nevertheless the old central-staircase plan stubbornly persisted in Devon towns, notably in Totnes and Barnstaple. The type continued even into the nineteenth century. Amory House, 11 St Peter Street, Tiverton, is a particularly attractive brick house of c. 1700 (6.14) and is one of the few houses in the town to survive the great fire of 1735. It is two rooms deep with a central staircase. Amory House also incorporated other interesting plan elements. By then kitchens were usually built in the main house but mostly at ground floor level. Here, however, the kitchen was placed in the cellar which is very rare before the Georgian period. Also the main front doorway does not lead to a passage. Instead there is a carriageway through the left end. No. 5 The Close, Exeter, built about the same time, has a rear-corner staircase off a similar side carriageway. In both cases the fronts are otherwise symmetrical.

Thus the late seventeenth- and early eighteenth-century town house employed a variety of plan forms of which the rear staircase plan was but one (6.4). At the same time the trading wealth of the period generated a boom in the building trades; the evidence is there in the great amount of work surviving from the time throughout Devon. If the town houses were not completely rebuilt they were usually given expensive modernizations. For instance the Manor House, Cullompton, (Thomas Trock's fine house of 1603; see 5.15 and p.111) was refurbished to a high standard in 1721 including new panelling, plasterwork and a handsome brick stair block. There are many newly built houses of the period in most Devon towns, a lot of them very difficult to recognize because they are disguised by later modernization. However there are two late seventeenth-century developments which deserve special attention and rank as of national importance.

The Strand, Topsham

The small town of Topsham, used since Roman times as the main port on the Exe, appears to have been virtually rebuilt between c. 1660 and 1730, and a remarkable number of houses still survive from this period. The town can boast perhaps the most attractive street of late seventeenth-century mercantile house in England; these are the so-called 'Dutch' houses of the Strand on the southern edge of the estuary (6.8).

In their original form these houses are similar in scale and they share a distinctive layout and appearance which suggests they were built as some form of controlled development. Unfortunately no original documentation survives from any of the houses, although a lease of 1776 abstracted from earlier documents suggests that No. 25, Topsham Museum, was built around 1689–90 for Joseph Hodder, the son of a sea captain.

Their plan-form is unusual and although no two are quite the same all share the same essentials (6.7). They are long buildings built gable-end onto the street, three or four rooms deep, and two storeys high with attics in the roof space, but their characteristic feature is that they have courtyards alongside separated from the street by tall brick walls containing large gateways. The Museum was extensively but superficially refurbished in 1739 but still provides a good example of the basic plan form. On the street front is a comfortable parlour. Behind is the entrance hall containing a fine staircase (6.9); the main doorway is off the

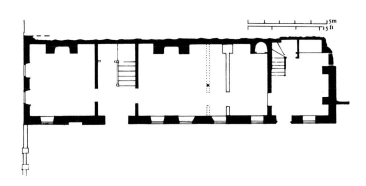

6.7. *No. 34 Strand, Topsham: ground-floor plan*

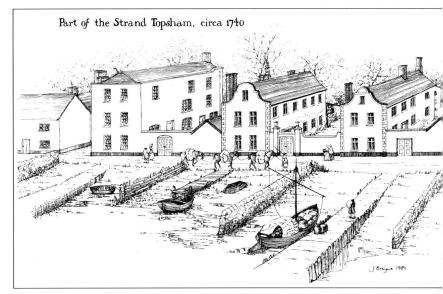

6.8. *A reconstruction drawing of part of The Strand, Topsham c. 1740. To left, No. 25 (the Museum) is depicted after its refurbishment in 1739. Nos 26 and 27 are restored to their late seventeenth-century form although the elegant eighteenth-century gateway to No. 26 is included.*

courtyard. Then there is the dining-room and at the back is the kitchen with a service stair. There is another well-finished room over the front parlour, either an upstairs parlour or principal bed chamber. Most of the other original Strand houses are variations on this pattern although a couple have kitchen crosswings returning across the courtyard. No. 41 is the largest of the houses and a little different as the end rooms here project forward as crosswings.

The gable-end fronts have distinctive curvinilear gables, and for this reason they have become known as the 'Dutch' houses. These gables are unique in Devon and because of Topsham's contemporary trading contacts with the Low Countries they have been attributed directly to Dutch influence. However, there is no evidence for a Dutch community in Topsham at the time and the interiors are wholly English. Moreover, such gables had long been in the repertoire of English architecture and there are many examples from the brick building areas of southern and eastern England.

Another distinctive feature of the Strand houses is the side courtyard and high front wall – a very unusual plan element without known parallels anywhere in England. It does have similarities to some houses of the sixteenth and seventeenth centuries in the Limburg area of the south-east Netherlands and in Alsace but these are too far inland to be seriously considered as the prototype for the Topsham houses. Unless parallels can be found from the Low Country ports the courtyard plan here on the Strand must be regarded as coincidental.

Bridgeland Street, Bideford

In contrast to the Strand in Topsham, Bridgeland Street in Bideford is very well documented. In 1690 Bideford was a prosperous and expanding port and the Feoffees (Trust Committee) of the Bideford Bridge embarked on a project to build a street of fine houses in order to profit from their rents. The *Bridge Trust Account Book* (preserved in the Devon Record Office[7]) records the acquisition of gardens, orchards, a carpenter's yard and the like between 1690–2 for building the 'Nue Street'. The development was to be tightly controlled and an entry of 30 March 1690 records a payment to Nathaniel Gascoyne, a carpenter, for 'drawing a designe of the Nue Street'. Jonathan Hooper's 1692 lease for 28 Bridgeland Street shows something of the building regulations:

Jonathan Hooper hath undertaken and promised that he ... will att his owne cost and charges within two yeares next

6.9. *A typical late seventeenth-century framed staircase from No. 41 The Strand, Topsham*

the wall upwards with good bricke, two storeys high and sixteen ffoote in breadth between the walls, the ffirst ffloore nyne ffoote in height and the walls thereof two bricks and a halfe in thickness, the second ffloore of the same height and two bricks thickness, all sealed and covered with slatt or helling stone from the quarries of Dennibowl ...

The *Trust Account Book* also records payment of £45 in 1690 to the brickmaker William Linex for building the 'drayne or common shore' down the street and in 1693 Nathaniel Gascoyne and William Linex were paid nearly £300 for building a 'Nue Kay or Slip' at the bottom of the street for the use of the tenants.

Most of these houses survive. It is an exceptionally fine group of contemporary houses although the first impression is of a street of nineteenth-century buildings. Only Jonathan Hooper's house, No.28, looks anything like it did originally from the exterior. Nevertheless many of the alterations are superficial, and, in several cases, mainly external. In fact most of the Bridgeland Street houses date from 1692–4 and some are remarkably well-preserved (plates 15, 20).

Although the houses vary in size they would have presented a unified frontage on each side of the street. They were built end to end, their fronts parallel to the street, two storeys high with attics and each has a symmetrical brick façade with a large central doorway. The plan (6.10) is based on a wide central cross-passage from the street to a rear courtyard which is connected to a fine dog-leg staircase. In all but one case (No.12; formerly known as the Great House) the stair is set at right angles to the passage. The main ground-floor rooms are invariably the kitchen, dining-room and parlour, and each house has a particularly fine first-floor room which is considered to be a principal parlour rather than a master bed chamber since it is the best room in the house. The variations in plan-form fall into two basic types. Firstly the L-plan house: a single-depth main block with parlour and dining-room either side of the central passage and a rear block behind the dining-room containing first the stairs then the kitchen. Secondly the double-depth plan house: dining-room with kitchen behind on one side of the passage, parlour with the staircase compartment behind off the other side of the passage.

Although the houses conform to these basic plan types no two houses are exactly the same. No.28, now the largest house on the street, has a full courtyard plan but is basically a variant of the L-plan house. The smallest of the original houses, the All Seasons

ensuing the date of theis present, erect and build a good and sufficient dwelling house on the said premises so allotted and sett out for him as aforesaid according to the course agreed, contayning sixtie two foote in ffront, well tymbered with oake and ffirre tymber, and foundation thereof layne with stone and so upwards in height two ffoote above the ground, the next of

public house, is a very compact version of the same layout. The Red House, Nos 25–26, is an interesting variation of the double-depth plan with its kitchen in a rear block.

The original leases also show that one plot on the street was set aside for a Nonconformist Church, the Great Meeting House. This was demolished in 1856 and replaced by the present Gothic Lavington Chapel but early nineteenth-century prints show a frontage very much like those of the other houses. A Meeting House on the best street in town is historically significant. It demonstrates that, in late seventeenth-century Bideford at least, the social and political disadvantages associated with Non-conformity earlier in the century had ceased to apply. The power and confidence of the Bideford merchants in the years immediately following the arrival of William of Orange had made Nonconformity not only respectable in Bideford, but also part of architectural identity of the finest part of the town. This comes through Daniel Defoe's report on Bideford after his visit there c. 1720.[8] He was impressed by 'a new spacious street ... as broad at the High Street of Excester, well built, and, which is more than all, well inhabited, with considerable and wealthy merchants, who trade to most parts of the trading world.' When describing the Meeting House Defoe commented favourably on the Clerk there, Mr Bartlett:

> A most acceptable gentlemanly person, and one who, contrary to our receiv'd opinion of these people, had not only good learning, and good sense, but abundance of good manners, and good humour; nothing soure, cynical or morose in him ... I wish I could say the like of all the rest of his brethren.

Conclusions

The purpose of this article is to highlight the importance of the great numbers of surviving town houses from the late seventeenth century and early eighteenth centuries in Devon. On the most basic level they are attractive buildings, hand-made by local craftsmen and impossible to reproduce in our times. As an historic resource they reflect an era of prosperity in this part of England, prosperity based on large-scale woollen cloth production and a maritime trade expanding to accommodate new colonial settlements. These houses rank as good, in some

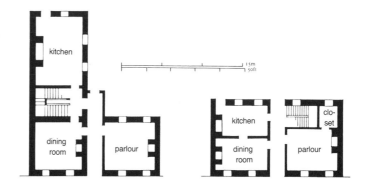

6.10. *Ground-floor plans at Bridgeland Street, Bideford; (left) No. 4, (right) No. 31*

6.11. *No. 12 Bridgeland Street, Bideford. Subsequent alterations to the façades of the houses in this street disguise their late seventeenth-century date.*

6.12 *Wooden bolection-moulded panelling over timber-framing from 10 High Street, Totnes.*

6.13. *Stucco fronts from 26 and 28 High Street, Totnes. The left house front has giant Ionic orders. The right house front has channelled rustication and keystones representing grotesque masks on the first floor.*

6.14. *Amory House, 11 St Peter Street, Tiverton. It has a panelled brick front with ogee-shaped window arches and a deep moulded timber eaves cornice.*

6.15. *Granite ashlar from Okehampton Town Hall*

cases better, as any other of their time and class in the country (plate 17).

The picture is one of variety. They are, as Michael Laithwaite says of the Totnes houses of the period, 'a curious mixture of national styles and local traditions'.[9] No other period in the history of English domestic architecture witnessed such a variety of appearance and plan-forms. Devon town house fronts were timber-framed, stone or brick; they were exposed, plastered, panelled or slate-hung; they were plain or ornamental. The house-plans are also varied but there is a unifying element. They expressed in their various ways different resolutions to the same set of expectations for a class of increasingly consumer-orientated people who would later be known as the middle classes. At this time their ideal house should provide a separate kitchen, dining-room, one or two parlours and several bed chambers (including a much higher standard of accommodation for servants than before); all built under the same roof with a maximum of comfort, privacy, and no less important, economy.

This was a period of change in all aspects of English life as the foundations were laid for a modern capitalist economy and a constitutional monarchy. Regional differences were under attack from improving communications and the circulation of cheap printed material to a population enjoying a relatively high level of literacy. The same influences were at work in domestic architecture and through this period Devon was increasingly tied into the national mainstream, but not yet slavishly following national pattern books. The strong traditions of the Devonshire craftsman survived and produced many fine buildings. Some, such as the groups on the Strand, Topsham and Bridgeland Street, Bideford, are of national importance. Others are of varying importance but still add interest and elegance to the Devon townscapes. They deserve more attention than they have enjoyed hitherto.

7.1. *Larkbeare House, Exeter*

7.2 *9 The Close, Exeter*
(top right)

7.3. *Law Chambers, Colyton*

7

Wall Painting and Lime-Plaster Decoration

JOHN THORP

This article describes the changing styles of internal surface decoration in Devon's historic buildings and concentrates mainly on the great period of Devonshire plasterwork. It is something of a tribute to Kathleen and Cecil French whose work in the 1950s did much to establish the national reputation of the local plasterers.[1]

Between 1500 and about 1730 there was a general rise in living standards throughout England and during this period Devon was a particularly prosperous county. No other county can boast so much or so great a variety of ornamental plasterwork from the sixteenth and seventeenth centuries. The wealth of decorative detail was apparently based on its large market. In most parts of contemporary England a luxury such as an ornamental plaster ceiling was generally reserved for the richest stratum of society but a strong economy in Devon supported a prosperous and increasingly acquisitive merchant and lower gentry class whose houses prove that they too aspired to such luxuries. The market even extended down to some of the yeoman farmers.

Interior decoration is very fragile. What survives is only a small proportion of what was originally created. When, for instance, James Crocker published his *Sketches of Old Exeter* in 1889, he included drawings of fourteen ornamental plaster ceilings from the sixteenth and seventeenth centuries; today only four of them survive. Interior decoration is also much more responsive to changing fashion than structural fabric. Although Devonshire plasterwork from this period displays a robust local identity it also shows that the local plasterers quickly adopted and assimilated the latest styles as they were developed in London and the great country houses.

At the beginning of this period (the early sixteenth century) architecture in Devon was still thoroughly Gothic. The ceiling from *10 The Close, Exeter*, (plate 18) is carved oak. The colouring is twentieth century.

Larkbeare House, Exeter, (7.1) was a fashionable mansion, probably built in the second quarter of the sixteenth century. Its ceilings were made up of richly-moulded intersecting beams with exposed joists. The roof structure was also exposed and backed with oak-boards. Lime plaster was used to skim over the masonry of the walls but essentially the structure was exposed and any decoration was carved onto it.

A fundamental change took place in the houses of the sixteenth century. They became much cleaner as the medieval open hearth fire was abandoned in favour of enclosed fireplaces with chimney stacks. With this came the widespread use of painted wall decoration. Most has been lost with the passage of time. The colours were crudely made and their fragile remains can very easily be overlooked and removed (particularly if whitewashed over). Pre-reformation examples are usually religious in character such as the painting of St Leonard from Dalditch Farm, East Budleigh or the stencilled symbols from *St Marys Cottage, Newton Poppleford* (plate 23), both of these painted onto oak plank-and-muntin screens.

In the second half of the sixteenth century, after the Reformation, more examples of decoration survive indicating an increased use of wall painting. Also the decorative repertoire was more varied and now usually secular in character. Renaissance style probably came through printed sources; Italian in origin but usually arriving in England second-hand through the Low Countries. For instance the 'grotesque' style was copied onto the window reveals and frieze in the hall of *St Nicholas Priory, Exeter*, probably *c*. 1580 (plate 24). What appears to have been some kind of reception room at *9 The Close, Exeter*, preserves most of a vigorous representation of Samson and the Lion, a popular allegoric motif in Devon (7.2). The master chamber at *Margells, Branscombe* has part of a stylized rural scene (plate 19). Cornucopias, mermen and the like figure on a painted oak

screen at Tudor Cottage, Sidmouth. The other side of this screen is painted with a royal arms in a strapwork pattern containing flowers. Early twentieth-century photographs in the Devon and Exeter Institution record a wall painting discovered during demolition of (probably) 69 High Street, Exeter: a painting of classical architecture with flowers and Latin texts. At the *Law Chambers, Colyton*, a parlour overmantel features a classical arcade in which each bay contains a female figure, each labelled in Latin and representing Experience, Good Reputation, Bad Reputation and Truth (7.3). This was probably part of a larger scheme.

Nos. 41 and 42 High Street, Exeter, were built as a pair of fashionable merchant's houses in 1564. The ceilings here were plastered but the main beams and timber-framing were still exposed. During its renovation in 1980 it was found that most of the principal rooms were decorated with bright colours. On the walls it was mostly vertical stripes with simple decorative friezes and the ceiling beams were painted with contrasting colours which picked out the chamfers or mouldings. Painting was also used here for architectural effect. For instance, a stone fireplace was painted red with white lines to simulate brickwork which was then extremely fashionable and a timber-framed partition was decorated to look like an oak panelled screen.

In the second half of the sixteenth century and into the seventeenth century the living standards of the gentry and merchant classes were rising and so too were their expectations of comfort and privacy. The medieval open hall had been abandoned in favour of heated parlours and bedchambers. The rooms were now well lit by large glazed windows. Increasingly the structural fabric was hidden; the ceiling beams with plaster, the walls with oak panelling, and the fireplaces were given ornamental chimney pieces or overmantels. The main hall of *Forde House, Newton Abbot* (plate 29), built for Sir Richard Reynell in 1610, is a fine example. It is lined with small field panelling; the staining is said to be based on traces found during renovation.

The art of ornamental plasterwork was revived in High Renaissance Italy whence it spread to France and England under royal patronage. Henry VIII's grand palace at Nonsuch may have been planned by Nicholas Bellin of Modena who had worked at Fontainebleau.[5] Excavations at Nonsuch have turned up many fragments of high quality stucco plasterwork from the inner court which was finished in 1540. It was a grand showpiece which greatly impressed visitors to the palace in the sixteenth and seventeenth centuries. Courtiers quickly followed and incorporated decorative plasterwork in their great provincial mansions and from there the craft spread down the social scale. Sir John Thynne's Longleat in Wiltshire probably provided much of the inspiration for decorative detail in south-west England. The earliest ornamental plasterwork in Devon comes from *Holcombe Court, Holcombe Rogus*. The Long Gallery ceiling (7.4) features a simple rib design including medallions containing letters which spell the name Roger Bluett. Presumably this and other contemporary plasterwork in the house, was installed before Sir Roger died in 1566. Even if it commemorates his death it is still amongst the earliest surviving ornamental plasterwork in Britain. Moreover, it is clearly the work of a local craftsman.

The execution and construction of the plasterwork developed from the native vernacular tradition of lime plaster rather than the continental stucco technique using plaster of Paris.[2] A Devon plaster ceiling was put up in the following manner. First, hand-riven oak laths were nailed to the underside of the joists or rafters leaving narrow gaps between them. Occasionally, as at Barrow Court, Somerset, water reeds were used instead of laths. A 20–40 mm. thick backing layer of cob plaster was laid under and pushed through the laths to hold it in place. This cob plaster was made of clay and sand bonded together with copious amounts of cow hair. Such cob plaster would retain its moisture for a long time which suited the plasterer when striking out his pattern. The ribs and any other mouldings were fashioned in the same cob plaster. They were hand-run *in situ* using moulding boards. Then the whole surface was given a 2–3 mm. thick skim of lime plaster. This was slaked lime which had been kept as 'putty' lime for between one and two years before use. It was mixed with silver or light coloured sand and bonded with some fine goats hair. Finally the lime plaster ornamentation was applied. Most of this was cast from moulds (probably carved beechwood) but the more expensive one-off creations were hand-fashioned *in situ*, although these too often included cast detail. Pendants were usually fashioned around a stout timber armature since they needed to be strong enough to carry a chandelier.

Two early plasterwork ceilings survive in west Devon. Both are by the same Devon plasterer and both are dated. *Collacombe Manor*, Lamerton, was enlarged and refurbished by Edmund Tremayne in 1574. He was a courtier (Clerk to the Privy Council) and had lived in exile in Italy in the 1550s. The hall (7.5) features not only a ribbed plaster ceiling with pendants, but also the Tremayne arms with its curious crest above the fireplace and an exceptionally fine royal arms over a covered dais canopy featuring a row of grotesque supporters. Edmund's brother-in-law, Sir Richard Grenville, converted Buckland Abbey, Buckland Monachorum, into his house in 1576. The ribbed plaster ceiling in the hall (converted from the old abbey church nave) is remarkably similar in style and detail to that at Collacombe Manor.

The next two examples of early ornamental plasterwork illustrated here are from town houses and show how quickly the richer merchants followed the lead set in the gentry mansions. The ceiling from *39 High Street, Totnes* (7.6) is one of several plaster ceilings on the same street which apparently date from the 1570s and 1580s. The other (7.7) is from the *Law Chambers, Colyton*. There is another early example at St Nicholas Priory, Exeter, (open to the public) which is dated *c.* 1580 because it includes the initials of William Hurst who bought the old Priory and converted it to a fashionable residence at around this time.

Right through the period ornamental plasterwork is commonly attributed to Italian, Flemish or Dutch craftsmen, but there is precious little evidence of this. The great majority of the work, if not all of it, is the product of Devonshire craftsmen. The inspiration was undoubtedly foreign but much of the early decoration is more closely related to English Tudor Gothic rather than the Renaissance style. The simple rib patterns draw their inspiration from timber prototypes, the pendants from fan vaulting. The moulded ornamentation features simple fleur-de-lys, Tudor rose motifs and small leafy angle sprays.

In the last years of the sixteenth and the early seventeenth centuries ornamental plasterwork proliferated in the houses of the gentry, merchants and more successful yeoman farmers. The style flourished with a greater complexity of rib pattern and more variety of increasingly ornate angle sprays. The ceilings from *Clysthayes, Silverton*, (plate 26) and from *Westacott, North Tawton*, (7.8) both date from around the turn of the century.

7.4. Holcombe Court, Holcombe Rogus

7.5. Collocombe Manor, Lamerton

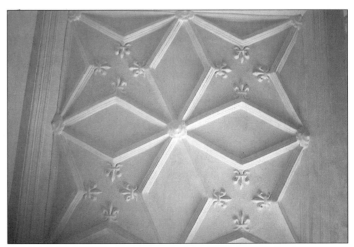

7.6. 39 High Street, Totnes

7.7. Law Chambers, Colyton

7.8. *Westacott, North Tawton*

7.9. *Dunsmoor, Silverton*

7.10. *Forde House, Newton Abbot*

7.11. *Forde House, Newton Abbot*

Jacobean plasterwork is characterized by its ambitious conception, lavish decoration and accomplished execution. The best (and there is plenty to choose from in Devon) bears comparison with any in contemporary England. The enriched broad rib arrives as early as 1610 in the great first floor chamber (probably Sir Richard Reynell's reception room and now called the Music Green Room) at *Forde House, Newton Abbot* (7.10), and about the same time in the parlour of the Grange, Broadhembury. In such ceilings moulded ribs enclose a strip of repeating decoration, most commonly a running vine but often including flowers and other fruits. An enriched rib ceiling was clearly a more expensive option since both these houses contain contemporary single rib ceilings in rooms of lesser status. Green, Bishopsteignton, is a small house and here the parlour ceiling of 1615 features single rib patterns either side of a central enriched rib pattern. Here the oak crossbeams are exposed but moulded and carved to emulate moulded plaster; they were probably lime-washed originally. Another option introduced in the early seventeenth century was the hollow rib ceiling like the one at *Dunsmoor, Silverton* (7.9) where the double moulded ribs have no cast ornamentation.

Single, hollow and enriched rib ceilings were made in great numbers up until the Civil War in the 1640s.

The decorative repertoire of the various Devon plasterers increased substantially between the closing years of the sixteenth century and *c.* 1640. Their sources were eclectic. Some Tudor motifs, notably the fleur-de-lys, retained their popularity. However more and more Renaissance motifs were employed, the style popularized through engraved plates in printed books like those by Abraham de Bruyn (published in 1581) and Henry Peacham (1612).[5] Imported luxury goods such as jewellery, silverware, embossed leather, tapestries, Persian carpets and the like circulated a miscellany of decorative motifs. There was great interest in fabulous and exotic birds and beasts in this age of discovery and in addition there were the flora and fauna of the English countryside. The strapwork cartouche was developed from engravings and was soon established as the most common feature of the better plasterwork. It is well represented at *Forde House*. The tympanum (7.11) in the chamber over the hall (now called the Charles I room) has a fine strapwork cartouche enriched with swags of fruit around the image of a mermaid holding a comb and mirror. The enriched rib ceiling of the Music Green Room (7.12) includes a series of cartouches mostly featuring fabulous creatures. The angle sprays here are larger than their Tudor antecedents. Although they draw inspiration from Renaissance arabesques they have been transformed at the hand of the local craftsmen, the classical, antique and grotesque elements have been replaced by mostly English flowers and fruits. The repeating frieze of female caryatds and arabesques is closer to Renaissance sources.

Forde House also illustrates a couple of other points. Firstly, the growing importance of the first-floor great chamber. Throughout the seventeenth century this room tended to be the most lavishly decorated room in the house. Secondly, the 'barrel-vault' type of ceiling continued its popularity throughout the first half of the seventeenth century. Its form provided opportunities for display, particularly of sumptuous pendants. Such ceilings naturally developed from the ceiling over of existing medieval roofs as at Hams Barton, Chudleigh (1621) and Rashleigh Barton, Wembworthy, but here at Forde House the roof was specially constructed for coved plaster ceilings over the first floor rooms.

Some of the finest plasterwork of this period comes from north Devon[6] and includes impressive enriched rib ceilings packed with cast, moulded and hand-wrought decoration. The magnificent plasterwork at *62 Boutport Street, Barnstaple* (plate 25) is dated 1620 and was created for the Guild of Spanish Merchants. Every panel is ornamented and together they provide a delightful menagerie and flower garden around four sumptuous strapwork cartouches, each featuring a scene from the Bible (7.13). A similar ceiling at Stafford Barton, Dolton, was removed there from a house in Barnstaple *c.* 1911. Another at *Rashleigh Barton, Wembworthy* (7.15) simply features birds, beasts and flowers.

Moulded plaster overmantels appeared with those early plasterwork ceilings of the 1570s in the gentry houses of west Devon. However they were rare before the 1590s. Most of those put up before the mid seventeenth century take the form of strapwork cartouches which appear on fireplace overmantels before they do in ceilings and tympani. One such overmantel at *Holcombe Court* (7.14) is dated 1591 and the arms in the cartouche commemorate the marriage of Roger Bluett and Elizabeth Chichester. Overmantels featuring armorial bearings

7.12. *Forde House, Newton Abbot*

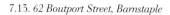

7.13. *62 Boutport Street, Barnstaple*

7.14. *Holcombe Court, Holcombe Rogus*

7.15. *Rashleigh Barton, Wembworthy*

survive in greater numbers than others from this period. A good example has been reset at *8 The Quay, Bideford* (7.16). It was erected for Sir Bevil Grenville and is believed to date from *c.* 1643. Royal arms tend to be restricted to the grander houses as, for instance, at Boringdon, Plympton St Mary, where there is a splendid example of *c.* 1640. The arms of Charles I are flanked by supporting figures representing Peace and Plenty, something of an act of faith so close to the outbreak of the Civil War!

Other overmantels of the period featured different displays, including some religious tableaux. A late Elizabethan overmantel at *Holcombe Court* (7.17) represents Moses and the Brazen Serpent. The modelling here as elsewhere, if not fine art, is vigorous, confident and charming. Another overmantel from the Dartmouth Butterwalk represents a New Testament scene, the Annunciation, flanked by two Old Testament figures, Moses and David. It is nearly half a century later and has no framing cartouche. Like the armorial overmantel at *Holcome Court* (7.14) many of the dated overmantels appear to commemorate weddings. A modest plaque dated 1637 at *Waye Barton, Chagford* (7.18) appears to be one such although the initials have not been identified. It is very unusual since it appears to record the age of each partner as well as the date and their initials.

The plasterers of the first half of the seventeenth century were mostly anonymous craftsmen. With the exception of the Abbott Pattern Book (described below) there is little documentary evidence from the period. Therefore the student of plasterwork must rely on what survives of the craftsmen's work. The rib patterns were laid out according to basic geometry and therefore could easily be copied. However the repeated cast detail, most obviously from the angle sprays and friezes, turns up time and again on different ceilings. They fall into distinct groups, each apparently belonging to a different family or guild business. The larger sprays and more complex friezes were often made from more than one mould and therefore elements were interchangeable, but never outside their group. These moulds were the plasterer's stock in trade and also their trademark. An intensive study of such detail could determine exactly how many 'firms' were working and how far they travelled in the South West. At present the evidence suggests three or four main 'firms' operating in Devon in the first half of the seventeenth century alongside several smaller, more local, enterprises.

One 'firm' which was by far the largest, was apparently responsible for most of the best plasterwork between *c.* 1600 and 1630, and probably introduced the enriched rib ceiling to Devon. Their work at Forde House, Newton Abbot and Green, Bishopsteignton has already been discussed. Other examples survive at The Grange, Broadhembury; Widworthy Court, Widworthy; Hams Barton, Chudleigh (1621); Bradninch Manor, Bradninch; Court Barton, Kentisbeare; and town houses in Exeter and Barnstaple. At present the 'showpiece' ceilings of north Devon cannot be firmly attributed to these plasterers because of the small amount of cast work employed. However it may be significant that the rear parlour ceiling at *62 Boutport Street, Barnstaple* is certainly their work (7.19). Maybe the hall ceiling was put up at the same time. Much Devon plasterwork, and particularly the north Devon work, is commonly attributed to the Abbott family who are known plasterers and were based near Bideford. However, as yet, no plasterwork before the 1670s can be proved to be their work and there was certainly more than one 'firm' working in north Devon at this time.

Another 'firm' was evidently based in the Dart valley and their distinctive set of moulds was used in most of the plasterwork in Totnes and Dartmouth of the 1630s and 1640s. The parlour ceiling of *64 Fore Street, Totnes* (7.21) is an example of their style. The richly ornamented soffit of the crossbeam is another feature of their work. Outside their base area they worked at 63 Woolborough Street, Newton Abbot, and 38 North Street, Exeter (parts of this ceiling are preserved in the Royal Albert Memorial Museum, Exeter). Perhaps their finest work was the Tree of Jesse ceiling (7.22) in the *Dartmouth Butterwalk*, a *tour de force* in a relatively small merchant's house of the period.

The one-off creations, like the overmantels, are more difficult to attribute to a school or 'firm' because they are mostly hand-wrought with little cast work. Styles can be copied. Moreover overmantels are not necessarily contemporary with ceilings in the same room and therefore might be done by different plasterers. There is nevertheless a series of overmantels from between *c.* 1590–1630 with striking stylistic similarities. They usually feature a coat of arms in a strapwork cartouche which is enriched with swags of fruit held on strings and naked putti figures (cherub-like figures), often sitting, and sometimes with sashes. The earliest of this group (7.24), now moved to *Widworthy Court,*

7.16. *8 The Quay, Bideford*

7.17. *Holcombe Court, Holcombe Rogus*

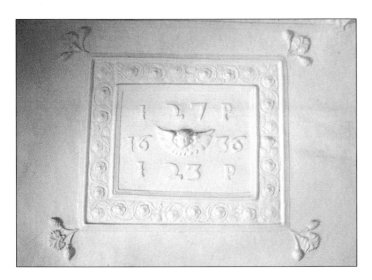

7.18. *Waye Barton, Chagford*

7.19. *62 Bourtport Street, Barnstaple*

Widworthy, is dated 1591 and here quaint squirrels sit on the outer scrolls of the cartouche. After *c.* 1600 most feature putti as, for instance, at *Walronds, Cullompton* (plate 22), which is dated 1605.

Iris Brook[7] has sought Italian influence from the fashions, and particularly the hairstyles, represented in the female figures used as brackets at *Widworthy Court* (7.23) and overmantel supporters at the Grange, Broadhembury (both *c.* 1600–1610). Both are associated with plasterwork of the largest Devon 'firm' and represent only a tiny proportion of their work; too little to propose the presence of a foreign craftsman.

Simple yet professionally made ornamental ceilings such as that from *Hill Farm, Christow* (7.20), show that the yeoman farmer class could afford good plasterwork in the first half of the seventeenth century. Obviously ornamental plasterwork was an indulgence for the best rooms of the house, usually the parlour or master bed chamber.

The 'summer parlour' at *Rashleigh Barton, Wembworthy* displays a most unusual ceiling (7.26). Each of the three bays features a free-flowing design of foliage issuing from a central coat of arms, and creatures as diverse as a garden snail and elephant inhabit the branches. This ceiling completely abandons the strictures of rib pattern. Other, more conventional plasterwork in the house dates from *c.* 1630. Maybe this is a little later in date. Even so it remain a unique and impressive testament to the versatility of the Devon plasterers.

With few exceptions sixteenth- and seventeenth-century plasterwork was originally lime-washed plain white. Its effect relied on the subtle interplay of reflected light and shadow. Sometimes a coat of arms was painted but most of these, too, were simply white. The overmantel from *Walronds, Cullompton* (plate 22) is an exception. It has been painted up on the evidence of traces of ancient colour although modern paints produce much stronger colours.

Decorative painting had not died out completely but there was apparently much less than in the sixteenth century. Surviving examples are rare. A painted fireplace of *c.* 1620–40 was discovered during the demolition of 38 North Street, Exeter. The design emulates a strapwork pattern of inlaid marble. Other seventeenth century fireplace lintels have been found with traces of colour but unfortunately none with a complete pattern.

Occasionally painted panelling has been found. A section from 72 High Street, Exeter (now in the Royal Albert Memorial Museum) has cream coloured arabesques on a maroon ground on each panel whereas the rails and muntins are bright yellow and rusticated with orange squiggles. Sometimes only the frieze of the panelling is painted. Some reset panelling at 9 The Close, Exeter, had a frieze painting of stylized interweaving foliage in the Renaissance manner.

The ferment and uncertainty of the Civil War brought about a hiatus in the building trades throughout England in the 1640s. Many of the great landowners were ruined by the troubles and even those who kept their positions avoided ostentatious expenditure. There is therefore very little plasterwork from the period. One exception is the sumptuous enriched rib ceiling of *c.* 1645 at Nettlecombe Court, Somerset, which is probably the work of a Devon 'firm' and another is the ceiling dated 1647 at Cleave Cottage, near Barnstaple. Both examples are thoroughly Jacobean in character.

The upheavals of the Civil War affected every aspect of life. When building activity began to pick up in the 1650s a new style was apparent, inspired for the most part by the genius of Inigo Jones and his revolutionary work for the court in the early seventeenth century. It arrived in Devon through *Forde Abbey* (now in Dorset but formerly Devon). Here, between 1655–58, Edmund Prideaux, the Attorney General, converted the old abbey on a lavish scale and with a style and quality which bears comparison with the other major English houses built in the 1650s. The design expresses a mannered classicism in a much purer form than had previously been seen in the South West.

One of the several contemporary ceilings in the house is illustrated (7.25). The spider web network of the rib pattern has been abandoned in favour of an overall concept of oval and rectangular panels. These are defined by massive beams with cornices of modillions, egg and dart and other purely classical motifs. Ornamentation is arranged around centrepieces and includes naturalistic wreaths of fruit and flowers, foliate scrolls, arabesques and masks. The plasterwork is recognizably the work of local plasterers. As usual it is commonly attributed to the Abbotts. Their lack of experience with pure classical detail shows through in the work. This spoils it in terms of fine art but even fine art purists have to admire its bold and sumptuous effect. The plasterwork of Forde Abbey marks the arrival of the new style.

7.20. *Hill Farm, Christow*

The Restoration in 1660 was evidently perceived as a return to 'normality' since building work in Devon took off apace against the background of a peace time local economy which was strong and growing. Bovey House, Beer, was refurbished in the 1660s and a panelled bed chamber was provided with an ornamental plaster ceiling in the new style. It celebrates the famous episode when the then Prince (now King) Charles escaped capture in Boscobel Wood by hiding in an oak tree. In the central panel his eyes and nose peep out from the foliage of the Royal Oak. Above the tree a winged angel head protects him while round the broad ribs Parliamentarian cavalry ride through the wood on their fruitless search.

The plasterwork here apparently emulates the Forde Abbey style but the ornamentation is very low relief and relatively crudely executed (the impression of the mould often shows around the features). The plasterers who made this delightful ceiling did not perhaps have the technical competence of the Jacobean masters but they certainly realized that fashions were changing.

The old style of rib pattern ceilings did not die out immediately. For example, at Rixdale in Dawlish, Thomas Trock refurbished his farmhouse in 1669. He too liked the image of Prince Charles in the Boscobel Oak which features on an overmantel. The ceilings, however, have single and enriched rib patterns; the style and motifs seem to be based on the plasterwork at Forde House, Newton Abbot, which was nearly sixty years old then, but is not as technically competent. Other ribbed ceilings were erected in the later seventeenth century and Cecil French reports a single rib ceiling dated 1726 at Yarner Cottage, Netherton, near Newton Abbot.[9] These early eighteenth-century ceilings often feature heart shaped panels along with initials and dates, apparently commemorating marriages. Two survive in the same house at Little Green, Shaldon; they are dated 1707 and 1716. A few, like that dated 1737 at Penstone Barton, Colebrooke, are done in mirror-writing and a mirror has been kept on the table below for as long as anyone there can remember.

Although most of the fine plasterwork right through this period is the work of anonymous craftsmen, much of the best of it is often attributed to the Abbott family who were based near Bideford. The business was started by one John Abbott in the 1570s. He was succeeded by his son Richard and then his grandson John.[10] John the younger (1639–1727) was certainly a renowned plasterer and there is good plasterwork attributed to him in contemporary accounts. Around 1700 he had his portrait painted holding a plastering tool. There also survives (in the Devon Record Office) the remarkable leather-bound pocket-size book known as the *Abbott Pattern Book* (7.27, 7.28).

The flyleaf is inscribed 'John Abbott his Booke 1665'. It includes more samples of his signature along with others of the same name but in different hands. The book opens with a series of late Elizabethan and Jacobean rib pattern designs; first for

7.21. 64 Fore Street, Totnes

7.22. Butterwalk Dartmouth

7.23. Widworthy Court, Widworthy

7.24. Widworthy Court, Widworthy

7.26. *Rashleigh Barton, Wembworthy*

7.25. *Forde Abbey, Dorset (formerly Devon)*

7.27. Page from the John Abbott Pattern Book

single rib ceilings and later including enriched rib or hollow rib designs. There follows a section on cartouches; many are strapwork but some are more classical. It features a royal arms dated 1662. Then a freer section features sketches of everyday, fabulous, exotic and allegorical creatures and includes a couple of Biblical compositions. It continues with a series of plaques with verses and finishes with a series of painted mural plaques along with detailed instructions for the preparation of oil and water colours.

The book is a wonderful resource. Close similarites occur between the examples drawn here and the details of the best plasterwork of the late Elizabethan and Jacobean period. The Abbotts were based in north Devon where the very best work was produced. It seems obvious to connect them. It has thus been considered a record of the Abbott family work over three generations. Maybe it is but the present writer has certain doubts. The flyleaf inscription claims that the book belonged to John Abbott the younger and was begun in 1655. He was then fifteen year's old; furthermore the sketches are somewhat childlike. It is worth considering whether or not the book was part of John Abbott's apprenticeship. Perhaps this involved a study of existing plasterwork; first ribs, then cartouches followed by modelled centrepieces. This might explain why there is no chronological sequence in the cartouche section. If so it may be that not all the plasterwork represented is actually Abbott work. The second half of the book is different. The decorative style is consistently late seventeenth century and it may be a pattern book.

In the second half of the seventeenth century plasterwork filtered down the social scale and examples can be found in surprisingly small houses. The quality is variable at this level. The master bed chamber at *Lewis Hill, Dunsford* is a delightfully rustic piece of work (7.29). Cecil French considered it sixteenth century,[11] but the structural evidence from the house suggests a date of *c.* 1660–1670. It appears to be the work of a local plasterer for someone who could not afford the professionals. Another relatively crude ceiling of similar date can be found at Rendells Down, Monkleigh.

Though technically crude, these ceilings are cherished today; many more must have been lost in the past two to three hundred years. The crudest example known to the author is now hidden at the Church House, Colebrooke, where a chamber ceiling has a frieze of finger-drawn St Andrew's crosses. Little Burn Farm,

Bickleigh, has two similar wall plaques, one dated 1664. Both feature a floral spray from the same cast used on several of the best early seventeenth-century ceilings. By 1664 they were old fashioned and presumably offered as a cheaper line.

The late seventeenth-century mainstream of English architecture and plasterwork was increasingly dominated by rich and well-travelled patrons with sophisticated tastes. London was emerging as an international metropolis and provided craftsmen of European class like Grinling Gibbons. The best plasterers, such as John Grove and Edward Gouge, worked with the leading architects of the day. Compared to their work the Devon plasterwork is vernacular; there are still those quirky touches that distinguish it as a regional style, although of a very high quality. Note, for example, the late seventeenth-century ceiling at *Youlston, Shirewell*, (7.30) distinguished by its unusually delicate ornamentation in high relief.

Exeter City Council accounts in the Devon Record Office record the payment in 1681 of £35 to John Abbott of Frithlestock for the plasterwork in the newly built *Customs House, Exeter Quay*. The main ceiling (7.31, 7.32) is a good example of his work in high relief ornamentation. The *Royal Hotel, Bideford*, incorporates a good late-seventeenth-century house, reputedly built in 1688 for the merchant John Davie. The ceiling here is even better (7.33) and is stylistically very similar to John Abbott's ceiling in Exeter.

There were other plasterers. Exeter Council paid the plasterer Thomas Lane £50 for a very fine ceiling of 1689 over the Apollo Room of the New Inn on Exeter High Street[12]. The ceiling no longer exists but it was recorded by James Crocker. Dr Portman comments on the expense of such ceilings by comparison with the estimated cost of £100 for the construction of a modest house on the outskirts of Exeter at the same time.[13] The Royal Albert Memorial Museum, Exeter, displays the corner cornice of another fine contemporary ceiling in the same style from the Half Moon Inn on Exeter High Street.

Following the Restoration the plasterer's craft took a while to re-establish itself in terms of quality and high fashion; but it did adapt and produced the second great period of Devonshire plasterwork between c. 1680–1720. The ceilings were still of lime-plaster construction but displayed a new, more sophisticated style. The ribs were now larger and defined simple symmetrical

7.28. *Page from the John Abbott Pattern Book*

7.29. *Lewishill, Dunsford*

7.30. *Youlston, Shirewell*

7.31. *Customs House, Exeter Quay*

7.32. *Customs House, Exeter Quay*

patterns around a large central panel; variously a circle, oval, quatrefoil or rectangle. The ornamentation was subjected to the overall concept and consisted of highly naturalistic foilage, fruits and flowers. The acanthus, the laurel and other classical motifs were introduced. Just about all the casts of the Jacobean period were now redundant since the new ornamentation is in high relief. To make a flower for instance, individually cast petals were fixed in shape around a wire armature which held it off the ceiling. An early example of the new style from Great Potheridge, Merton, probably dates from the 1670s. It is notable, being the only example in Devon where the central panels were painted.

The new style soon filtered down to affect most classes of house. These more modest ceilings emphasized different aspects. The row of late-seventeenth-century merchants' houses on the Strand, Topsham contains two simple but charming ceilings with high relief rib enrichment, the one illustrated is from *Shell House, Topsham* (7.35). Another Topsham house ceiling, from 28 Fore Street (1693), has an enriched rib oval but in low relief. The merchants' houses in Bideford's Bridgeland Street date from 1692–4. Several ceilings here have simple plain rib designs with acanthus leaf friezes. (See pp.123–5) for a fuller discussion of these houses at Topsham and Bideford. Sometimes ceilings feature high relief branches (usually oak or laurel), as at 52 High Street, Totnes (1694) or little floral sprays in the corners, as at 67 High Street, Exeter. Most common, particularly in the early eighteenth century, are simple rib designs maybe featuring central rosettes, for example, at *The Manor House, Cullompton* (7.34) from a renovation of *c.* 1721.

In the second half of the seventeenth century there was a fashion for lining the jambs, cheeks and backs of fireplaces with *sgraffito* plasterwork. This was made by laying an undercoat of slate-grey coloured plaster covered with a skim of lime plaster. The design was drawn on the surface and then highlighted by scraping parts down to the undercoat. This form of decoration is very fragile and can be so easily lost when an old fireplace is opened up. The fireplace at Gulliford Farm, Lympstone has a pretty design but usually simple geometric patterns are employed. Examples like these can be seen in the musueums at 33 St Andrews Street, Plymouth and 70 Fore Street, Totnes. *Sgraffito* plasterwork is used externally to embellish the frontage of 225–6 High Street, Exeter (plate 16).

Wressing Cottage, Kentisbeare has a use of plasterwork that is probably unique. A late seventeenth-century bible cupboard was given an architectural frame with a cherub head (plate 27).

Plaster overmantels with strapwork continued into the second half of the seventeenth century but were steadily superceded by more elegant cartouches like the one from *Woodlands, Little Torrington* (7.36). In fact plaster overmantels declined in popularity towards the end of the century. By this time the better rooms were usually panelled. The most common type had large fielded panels in two heights defined by bold 'bolection' mouldings. Usually the chimneypiece and overmantel were part of the panelling. Such panelling might be natural wood, stained, grained, or lime-washed. Sometimes the overmantel contains an oil painting; often a vaguely Italianate landscape, as in the example from *Countess Wear House, Exeter* (7.38).

It seems there was a revival of painted decoration in the late seventeenth and early eighteenth century. However, time and changing fashions have covered up most examples. Evidence often comes to light during demolition or building works. For instance, a report from 1926[14] noted that the parlour of 41 High Street, Exeter, was lined with canvas which was painted with a floral design, dating from *c.* 1720. During the demolition of 38 North Street, Exeter, a painted ceiling of *c.* 1690 was discovered; it showed clouds on a night sky with cherub heads and gold leaf stars. The head of a late seventeenth- to early eighteenth-century cupboard at *Pynes, Washford Pyne,* (plate 21) is painted with a colourful design around a smiling sun. John Abbott's Pattern Book includes detailed instructions for the preparations of oil and watercolour paints and a series of designs for painted mural plaques. These were apparently part of the plasterer's repertoire.

Only a handful of these plaques now survive although many more are probably hidden by later plaster and paint. Most painted plaques contain morally uplifting (usually biblical) quotations but a good example discovered during the demoliton of *Island House, Bideford* (7.37),[15] is more mundane and obviously identifies the building as a public house in the 1680s. The text reads:

> *My hearty guests you are welcome all*
> *If yar pay for what you call*
> *And if my pot seems to be small*
> *When there is noe excise ile pay for all*

7.33. *Royal Hotel, Bideford*

7.34. *The Manor House, Cullompton*

7.35. *Shell House, Topsham*

7.36. *Woodlands, Little Torrington*

yellow   maroon   red   blue   pale purple

0   10   50 cms

0   1   2 feet

1982

7.37. Island House, Bideford

7.38. *Countess Wear House, Exeter*

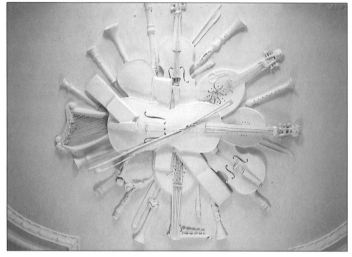

7.39. *28 South Street, Great Torrington*

7.40. *Lower Withecombe, Chagford*

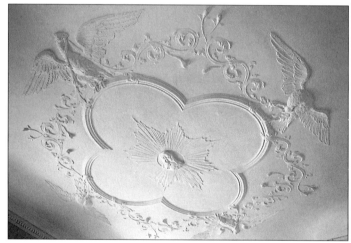

7.41. *The Priory, Totnes*

The plaque represents a current of folk art that existed alongside the fine joinery and plasterwork found in the houses of the rich before the era of industrial mass production. The inclusion of texts in these plaques illustrates the spread of literacy down the social scale in seventeenth-century England.

In the closing years of the seventeenth and early eighteenth century the best plaster ceilings developed theme features. The dining room ceiling at Bowringsleigh, West Avington, has the theme of war. It was erected c. 1697 for Sir William Ilbert. Cecil French reports a tradition that it was the work of Dutch craftsmen.[16] This is possible since several foreign master plasterers were working in England at the time[17] but if so, this is the exception. Most plasterwork was still recognizably the work of local craftsmen. The curious 'war' ceiling at Smallacombe, Lifton is certainly Devon work. So too is the early eighteenth-century ceiling at *Bellair, Exeter* (plate 28) and the 'music' ceiling at *28 South Street, Great Torrington* (plate 7.39) dated 1702.

By the 1720s and 1730s the decorative style was evolving towards the rococo. Plaster ornamentation returned to low relief and there was less of it. The impression is of grace and freedom. The ceiling from *The Priory, Totnes* (7.41) from c. 1730 features a starburst badge containing a bearded head in profile in a quatrefoil panel, each segment crowned with an elegant eagle with flowing scrolled foliage. Dartmouth Customs House has a ceiling in the same style from c. 1739, but the most impressive example of the style is probably from the Dartmouth Mansion House (c. 1736) where the stair-hall and first floor are packed with classical allegories. This stage marks the end of the great period of Devonshire plasterwork. Fine quality work continued to be produced and most was still the work of local men, but the craft had been absorbed into the national mainstream. It had lost its distinct regional identity

8

Recent research projects in Devon

JO COX AND JOHN THORP

The first edition of *Devon Building* was published in 1990 and research since then has further enlarged the picture it painted of Devon's traditional architecture. Many more houses and farm buildings have been recorded and analysed, strengthening the outline of what is already known and providing new detail that comes from the unique history of each building. More extensive projects have looked at building types within particular areas of Devon, shedding light on patterns of traditional building that vary from one part of the county to another. These projects include Isabel Richardson's survey of vernacular buildings for the National Trust, Susanna Wade Martin's survey of farm buildings for Devon County Council and English Heritage, and Robert Waterhouse's on-going research into larger medieval houses of the South Hams. Three particular areas of research, funded by English Heritage and Devon County Council, illustrate some of the progress made in understanding key aspects of traditional building since 1990. Each relates to building materials, although in rather different ways. In each case the work served to emphasize the vital links between local building traditions and the exploitation of the Devon landscape.

Firstly, dendrochronology – accurately dating timber on the basis of growth rings – has begun to refine and, in some cases correct, the dates of individual vernacular houses in the county which were previously dated largely on the basis of their style, particularly that of their roof carpentry. The Devon dendrochronlogy project has also revealed a curious gap in domestic building activity (which has parallels in other counties) between about 1340 and 1450. Fast-grown oak was found in many Devon houses. This has made successful timber sampling difficult but, in turn, demonstrates remarkable skills in woodland management in the county in the medieval period.

Secondly, Devon combed wheat reed thatching is now understood in more detail than in 1990. Botanical analysis of samples taken from ancient thatch surviving in Devon roofs has shed light on the cereals (and other materials) used for roofing. Documentary research reveals that while Devon is remarkable for thatch today, it was not the only county with an abundance of straw roofs. Straw thatch, a natural by-product of grain-growing, was the commonplace roofing in southern England before c. 1800. Devon's economic history, however, created the ideal circumstances for its survival, in contrast to losses in other regions.

Thirdly, the story of the local slate roofing tradition is now clearer too. Small random-width slates, laid in diminishing courses to make a roof of pleasingly small-scale texture, were used extensively for roofing from at least the fourteenth to the mid-nineteenth century. The relatively small size of the slates used for roofing exploited as much as possible of the material that could be won from the county's slate quarries. In the late nineteenth century the Devon quarries were slowly squeezed out of business by competition from Wales.

The Devon Dendrochronology Project

Until recently, the dating of vernacular buildings in Devon was largely based on stylistic criteria, since old deeds or other documentary material hardly ever mention the construction of new houses or other buildings. Such dating was essentially a matter of interpretation based on experience, taking into account the layout of the building and the details of its construction and comparing these with other, similar houses. With the earlier buildings of Devon it is usually the roof carpentry, often the most readily visible, unaltered part of a medieval house, which is the main focus of any discussion of dating. For instance, the jointed cruck roof truss which is so typical of early Devon houses, clearly evolves from forms with the joint secured by face pegs, to the later, ubiquitous type using side pegs. Similarly, ridges are first set square, but later are turned so their faces are parallel with the slope of the roof and its rafters (8.1, 8.2). All these features are known to be medieval since the roof timbers are commonly encrusted with soot indicating that they were over an open hall heated by an open hearth fire. Nevertheless this does not provide an absolute date. Now, however, the understanding of historic buildings is being revolutionised by the application of a scientific dating method known as dendrochronology, or tree-ring dating, which is providing those elusive absolute dates for the construction of historic buildings.

Tree-ring dating makes use of the way that most trees in temperate regions grow by putting on annual growth rings under the bark. There are various genetic and environmental factors which determine the thickness of the growth each year but the major determinate is the weather. The tree will put on a wide ring in a year of favourable growing conditions but a narrow ring in a poor year, such as the drought year of 1976. Thus an examination of the pattern of annual growth rings may reveal both the age of the tree and evidence of the fluctuating climatic conditions apparent during its lifetime.[1]

Trees of the same species within the same region will show similar patterns of growth. Therefore if the tree-rings of several recently-felled oak trees are measured and plotted carefully the graphs produced will match. Furthermore, because the sequence follows the unpredictable course of the weather there is only one true position of match. Most older buildings in England use oak for the main structure and so it is oak which has been studied. By overlapping successively older samples of oak it has been possible to build up a tree-ring chronology for Great Britain as a whole from the present back to 4989 BC (with a gap in England in the 4th century AD), and in Northern Ireland back to 5452 BC.[2]

By this method it is possible to measure the tree-ring sequences from historic oak timbers in ancient roofs and match them to established tree-ring chronologies. This can date the timbers very precisely. If they preserve, in places, the outer sapwood rings up to the bark-edge it is possible to establish the felling date of the trees cut down to build the roof, or indeed any other historic oak feature, even down to the season of the

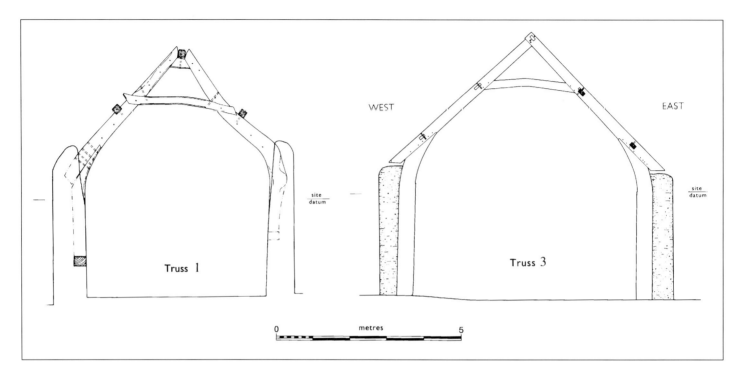

8.1. *The oaks for the roof of Chimsworthy, Bratton Clovelly, were felled in 1307. The left-hand principal rafter is a face-pegged jointed cruck, a simple scarf joint at the elbow. The other principal is a true cruck. The ridge at the apex is square-set and sits on a yoke between the principals.*

8.2. *The barn roof at Prowse Farm, Sandford, produced a felling date-range between 1483–c. 1490. The trusses here are all standard side-pegged jointed crucks, that is to say, the post has a tenon along its top edge to engage the underside of the principal. The ridge is set diagonally in the same plane as the rafters.*

year. Since most historic houses were built of freshly-cut green oak, the date of construction was very likely to be within the year following the felling of the tree. Thus the felling date produced by dendrochronology can be assumed to be the date of construction.

Although it is possible to cross-match the tree-ring curves (the superimposed plots from several trees or timbers) from a Devon site to chronologies established elsewhere in England, there is a high failure rate. Given oaks of a decent age, of a minimum of eighty years or older, those from the same woodland or parish are mostly easy to match, but the further away the comparisons are made, the more difficult matching becomes. There were some successes in the 1980s and early 1990s in applying dendrochronology to buildings in the county, notably the early fourteenth century roof at Exeter Cathedral, but more failures. As opposed to a national success rate of 72 per cent, the success rate in Devon was 21.5 per cent, if Exeter Cathedral is excluded, where the success rate was 47 per cent.[3] For this reason Devon County Council and English Heritage commissioned a pilot dendrochronology project in Devon in order to attempt to establish a local tree-ring chronology. This was carried out between 1995–97. Twenty historic roofs were selected by Cathy Groves of the University of Sheffield Dendrochronology Laboratory on the basis that each was constructed from several different oak trees and that the trees were reasonably old, that is to say containing eighty or more tree-rings. At least eight samples were taken from each roof using a specially adapted drill (8.3), which produced pencil-sized cores that could be examined back at the laboratory. At the same time the roofs were surveyed by Keystone Historic Buildings Consultants so that the dendrochronological evidence could be related properly to the standing structure.

The results were promising but incomplete. It was exciting to discover that the oldest of the twenty, Old Cheriton Rectory at Cheriton Bishop produced a felling date of 1299–1300 (8.4). Although this is amongst the oldest domestic roofs so far discovered in the South West, its cruck construction was sophisticated, indicating an already mature tradition. Also, a group of stylistically early roofs with square-set ridges were found to date from the first half of the fourteenth century. These nicely matched up with a chronology established from samples taken from Exeter Cathedral roof. Such dates were earlier than any building historian had dared to suggest. For instance the impressive roof at Rudge, Morchard Bishop, was constructed from oaks felled in 1316, compared to the date of c. 1425 given to it on stylistic grounds by Charles Hulland in his excellent article on the old farmhouses of mid and north Devon.[4] As might have been expected, all the side-pegged jointed crucks with diagonal ridges produced dates from the second half of the fifteenth century and the sixteenth century.

However nine of the twenty roofs failed to date. In a couple of cases failure was because the timbers contained insufficient tree-rings, but another two produced curves which cross-matched with each other but not with any established master chronology, and another three produced respectable site chronologies which were also undatable. Moreover it seems that there is a gap in the chronology. Dates have been produced from before c. 1340 and from after c. 1440 but none of the roofs sampled during the project produced a date from the intervening period. One possible explanation for this might be a hiatus in building work following the ravages of the Black Death in Devon in the 1340s but the evidence from the core samples suggests otherwise. The timbers from the early fourteenth century were commonly from oaks which had been cut down when they were about a hundred years old, and so too were the oaks used in the late fifteenth century roofs. Had there been a period where no buildings were being erected one

might expect the later medieval trees to be up to two hundred years old. Furthermore several of the roofs which were sampled but failed to date might be considered to be late fourteenth or early fifteenth century on stylistic grounds. In short, more work is required to create a master chronology for Devon which will help date historic roofs. The success rate of dating historic structural timbers was 55 per cent during the Devon Dendrochronology Project, but has since fallen to 45 per cent. This can be explained by the fact that the buildings in the project were specifically chosen in order to try and build up a Devon master chronology, whereas those sampled since were chosen by English Heritage simply as important historic buildings for which they sought a firm date.

In those cases where the timbers have been well-trimmed and the sapwood has been lost only a date-range, rather than a precise felling-date, can be expected, like the tiny two-room open hall house in Sandford, known as Ivy Cottage, which was dated 1538–58. Even so, this is far more precise than a date obtained from stylistic evidence only.

Another aspect of dendrochronology is the light it sheds on ancient woodland management. It is a remarkable fact that many of Devon's medieval houses were built of fast-grown oaks. It seems that the medieval woodsman was able to manage oaks so that they would grow to a decent building size (producing 310mm or 1 foot square timbers) in 30–40 years. In modern managed woodland this would take over 100 years. How this was done is a matter of speculation at present. The growth rate was prodigious, producing very fat annual rings but, unfortunately, too few to produce a dating by dendrochronology. During the course of the Devon Dendrochronology Project it was often the case that two, three or sometimes four farmhouses had to be visited before one was found with sufficient tree-rings to merit sampling. The new, reliable dates for the timbers also show how woodland management apparently improved through the late medieval period. Many of the timbers used in the early fourteenth century roofs were of insufficient length for their purpose and were made up of two pieces scarfed together, as can be seen at Old Cheriton Rectory (8.4). Others were irregular and evidently difficult to fashion in the required shape, as at Chimsworthy in Bratton Clovelly, where the oaks for the roof were felled in 1307 (8.1). By con-

8.3. *Cathy Groves of the University of Sheffield Dendrochronology Laboratory sampling the roof timbers of a seventeenth century roof at Chaffcombe Manor, Down St Mary.*

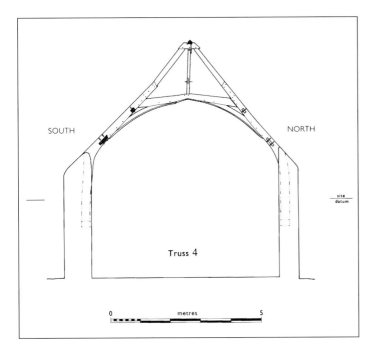

SOUTH

NORTH

site
datum

Truss 4

0   metres   5

8.4. *Old Cheriton Rectory, Cheriton Bishop, is the oldest roof so far discovered in Devon. The oak trees used in its construction were felled in the winter of 1299–1300. Since houses were then built of green oak it is very likely that the house was built AD 1300.*

trast most late fifteenth century roofs are made up of regular timbers, as for instance in the barn at Prowse Farm, Sandford, where the timbers produced a felling date-range of 1483–c. 1490 (8.2). This would seem to imply that the early roofs came from oaks growing in wild woodland, whereas the oaks for the later roofs were from managed woodland. This is in itself a fascinating but separate area for historic research.

Dendrochronolgy is also proving that the kind of good quality straight-grained oak required for boarding or joinery in Devon from the medieval period onwards was likely to have been imported from the Baltic area, whilst the basic constructional timbers were home-grown. At Bowhill, a gentry mansion built on the outskirts of Exeter in the early years of the sixteenth century, the boards for the oak ceiling in the parlour were of Baltic origins.[5] Future work could involve sampling pine, which was also imported into Devon and used in buildings from the middle of the seventeenth century onwards. Elsewhere, for instance in Cornwall, imported Baltic and Scandinavian pine has been dated by reference to the pine master-curves produced in the countries of origin.

In conclusion, tree-ring dating offers a probability of dating houses absolutely, provided the timbers are suitable for sampling, but it also raises new questions relating to both historic woodland management and the historic trade of timber within regions and between countries. The potential for dendrochronology is enormous in Devon. In particular its ability to provide reliable dates for local historic buildings will prove a tremendous boon for those studying building history.

Devon Thatch

In the early 1990s English Heritage funded a series of research projects on English thatching. These were commissioned as a result of growing concern that historic regional variation in thatching was disappearing. Since c. 1945, the speed of change to a roofing system that was still very much in use had blurred a good understanding of which methods and materials were peculiar to any one region or part of a region. In Devon, the change had been one from straw thatch to water reed. The research projects were given impetus from the work of John Letts, an archaeo-botanist. In 1992 Letts recognised that historic straw thatch preserved under newer layers was the major surviving resource in Europe for the study of medieval plant remains. Letts' work was disseminated in a number of publications.[6] Using the results of this research, in 2001 English Heritage published advice on how types of historic thatch might best be conserved, *Thatch and thatching: a guidance note.*

Devon is unrivalled in England for thatched roofing. It has more thatched buildings than any other county, although this is only a fraction of what once existed. The traditional method of rethatching is to 'overcoat' old straw thatch on houses with new, rather than stripping the roofs back to the timbers at a rethatch. This has left a legacy of layers of historic thatch underneath modern overcoats. The new coat was traditionally fixed to the old with 'spars', U-shaped staples of split hazel, twisted in the middle, with sharpened ends. Although the overcoating system was, and still is, not peculiar to Devon, the county preserves a uniquely rich inheritance of thatch dating from the period of open hall houses. This is the original medieval thatch put on when the house was first constructed. It is blackened, like the roof timbers that support it, from the smoke of the open hearth fire (plate 2). Amongst the many houses in rural Devon that originated as open hall houses, about 180 have been identified with smoke-blackened thatch and there are undoubtedly more to be found.

The significance of smoke-blackened roof timbers and smoke-blackened thatch as evidence for the open hall phase of Devon houses was first published by Michael Laithwaite and N.W. Alcock in 1973 in a seminal article on Devon's medieval houses.[7] More smoke-blackened thatch was identified in the listing resurvey of Devon rural buildings in the late 1980s, although identification depended on whether fieldworkers had access to the roof spaces of the houses that were visited.

For an archaeo-botanist accustomed to analysing tiny fragments of plant material from excavated sites, the realization that some English thatched roofs contained literally tons of crops grown in the late medieval period, was an overwhelmingly exciting discovery. Devon has more by far of these roofs than any other county. John Letts' analysis of samples of thatch taken from Devon smoke-blackened roofs was combined with research into the history of cereals. This revealed new and, compared with written records, direct information about what was growing in Devon's fields (including weeds) in the late medieval period. Rye and bread wheat were the most common plants, but these were not the pedigree varieties bred since the nineteenth century. They were taller and less uniform. Only successful plants could be used for seed-corn for the following year's crop and, over time what was grown in Devon would have become adapted to the local conditions.

Letts' work also clarified the antiquity of the combed straw method of thatching in Devon. Today this is known as combed wheat reed. This is a tradition that can be traced back to the medieval period and is shared with other South West counties. Care was taken when processing the straw from field to roof to ensure that it remained in bundles with all the ears at one end, and the butt ends of the straw (which are visible on the outside of a thatched Devon roof) at the other. Threshing methods were employed that kept the stems unbruised. On the roof this allowed the stiff straw to be dressed into position using a tool.

The underside of smoke-blackened combed straw thatch is a revelation of the quality and variety of Devon thatch craftsmanship in the fourteenth, fifteenth and sixteenth centuries. Today we may only have a 'short' view of the roof, balanced on the upperside of an inserted ceiling rather than from the floor. However, it is still an unparalleled view of one major element of a house – the roof – as it was seen by the medieval users of the house.

In many cases there can be no doubt that the thatcher laid his material with an eye to pattern and decorative effect. A layer of straw, often rye (which has more wiry stems than modern wheat), may be laid over the wide oak laths at right angles to them, with remarkable care and neatness, preventing any odd straws from the rest of the coat poking through. The straw above was attached to the roof construction by ties round the rafters. These are often at regular intervals and make a unified pattern of their own. It is difficult to imagine how this could have been achieved without an assistant thatcher working inside the roof and passing the tie, secured in a needle, back out to a partner on the outside of the roof. The materials used as ties are a reminder of the ingenuity with which local resources were exploited. Hazel, probably from managed woodland, can be found, twisted to make it pliant. Twisted straw rope was also used, as were wild hedgerow plants, Honeysuckle and Old Man's

Beard, selected for suppleness. If the underside of some smoke-blackened thatched roofs reveals intricate visual refinement, others are more rustic, even where the roof carpentry has a superior finish. Wattling is found in association with (for Devon) an unusually elaborate roof with cusped wind-braces at Tytherleigh Cott, Chardstock.

The quality of Devon houses of open hall origins with smoke-blackened thatch corrects any assumption that straw was then a poor man's roofing material. In the sixteenth and seventeenth centuries new rural houses were built with chimneys and two storeys throughout and the old open hall houses were modernised to match. Nevertheless, thatch continued to be an acceptable roofing on these buildings (Plate 5), as well as on those of lower status and on farm buildings. It was found then (and has survived today) on the most up-to-date and substantial farmhouses, and excluded only from the very largest mansions.

The decline in Devon's economy in the late eighteenth and nineteenth centuries, relative to its buoyancy in the sixteenth and seventeenth centuries, had benefits for the survival of thatched roofing. Thatch was replaced by slate in the smaller towns but it held up in rural Devon. There was little of the competition from other roofing materials that replaced thatch in industrialised and more urbanised counties. Devon was slow to take to the widespread use of threshing machines, which crushed straw along its length and made it unsuitable for the Devon method of thatching. The combed straw tradition stubbornly kept hold in the county, helped along by the development of machinery expressly designed to comb straw for thatching. A reed comber that could be attached to a standard threshing machine was invented and built in Braunton in the late nineteenth century and variations on this device are still used today for producing thatching straw.

To date no compelling evidence has been found to establish the use of water reed for Devon thatched roofs before the nineteenth century. One example of smoke-blackened water reed was found by Letts in Otterton, but this was used only as the thin layer on the roof timbers to support blackened straw thatch above. There is documentary evidence of small quantities of water reed cut for thatching in the South Hams in the late nineteenth century. Since c. 1950 water reed, imported from abroad, has been used extensively in the county. Devon thatchers use it as an 'overcoat', whereas in the water reed areas of Norfolk and Suffolk it is commonly used as single coat, the material being stripped back to the roof timbers at every rethatch.

Developments in the modern grain industry have not been kind to straw thatch. Thatching straw cannot be produced from a field harvested with the combine harvester. Wheat breeding programmes have reduced the length of straw. Complex regulation, both national and European, is an obstruction to maintaining or experimenting with old varieties of wheat in order to discover the ideal straw from a thatcher's point of view. Nevertheless, some Devon farmers, sometimes in partnership with thatchers, continue to grow good quality thatching straw as a specialised crop. This is a valuable element within the county's beleaguered farming industry and produces, out of Devon's fields, a sustainable, energy-efficient roofing which has been a living tradition in the county since before the early fourteenth century.

Traditional slate roofs in Devon

Before the late nineteenth century, slate was the principal alternative roofing material to thatch in Devon.[8] It was more durable and represented less of a fire risk, a real advantage in towns. What survives of traditional Devon slate roofing today is mostly nineteenth century, but documentation and archaeology establish a continuity from the medieval period.

The traditional Devon slate roof is composed of small slates of random width and length which are laid in diminishing courses from eaves to ridge (1.13). The slates were mostly roughly shaped, approximately rectangular or slightly tapered. They were either hung over riven oak laths or, from the late seventeenth century, sawn softwood battens. Slates hung over laths have what is usually a single hole near the top to take a wooden peg, the origin of the local name 'peggies' for Devon slates. The horizontal uniformity of each course was achieved by making the hole the same distance from the bottom edge or 'tail' of each slate in the course. In each course, some slates may be somewhat longer than others. Slates cut to inexact sizes can be holed and top-hung to produce regular coursework, the irregular headers being lost from view.[9]

Peggies were usually laid in conjunction with lime plaster. This was applied in a band over each course or as blobs on each slate, so that slates laid in the course above could be pressed down into it (8.5). This lime plaster bedding protected the slates from being lifted off the roof in severe wind and prevented rattle. It also meant that if the odd peg failed, the slate was attached to its neighbour above and below and was unlikely to fall. The system of diminishing courses meant the eaves, subject to a greater flow of water than the courses close to the ridge, were given extra protection by having fewer joints. The use of very large slates nailed to the rafters at the eaves and verges, which can be seen on some surviving pegged slate roofs in the county, seems to be medieval in origin and provides a pleasing visual 'border' at the outside edges of the roof (8.6). Large slates at the eaves and verges were not confined to slate roofs. Engravings and photographs show that they were sometimes used in conjunction with thatch.

In addition to using lime mortar between the courses, surviving late eighteenth and nineteenth century pegged slate roofs show variations on using lime mortar on the underside. A mortar fillet may be laid over the upper edge of the laths, between lath and slate. Plastering between the laths and across the underside of the slates is another technique. Sometimes the plaster completely obscures the laths and sometimes it is no more than a fine smear over them and they are easily visible.[10] Pointing slate roofs from above was one method of maintenance. An extreme version was a slurry of lime plaster over the whole of the outside of the roof. The modern version is a cement slurry or tarred finish, the latter making re-use of the slates virtually impossible. Celia Fiennes, writing of Plympton in the 1690s was taken with the combination of slate and lime she saw and described the town as:

'....all built of stone and the tyleing is all slatt, which with the lime its cemented with makes it look white like snow, and in the sun shineing on the slatt it glisters...'[11]

Some pegged slates may have been pegged into pre-drilled holes in boards, fixed over the rafters. This has been recollected by one Devon craftsman and boards with holes have been noted in some Devon church roofs, although these may have been designed for oak shingles.

8.5. *Pegged slates bedded in lime mortar.*

8.6. *A pegged slate roof with larger slates at the eaves and verges on a farm building at Haye Farm, Ludbrook. The house is dated 1817 and this is the probable date of the farm buildings.*

The distribution of slate roofing across the county is far more complex than the distribution of thatch. The West Country has two geological bands of slate that have been exploited for building materials. The first runs roughly west-east, extending from Delabole in north Cornwall eastwards across to Newton Abbot and down to Kingsbridge. The band is interrupted by Bodmin Moor in the west and the south of Dartmoor in the east. There is a second band to the north extending eastwards from Mortehoe in north Devon to the Brendon Hills and Huish Champflower in west Somerset.

The output of material from the Devon quarries was not only roofing slates. Blocks which could not be split thinly went for walling-stone, hearthstones, flooring slabs, shelving and cisterns, as well for as church monuments and the slate headstones with their beautifully-lettered inscriptions found in many Devon churchyards. John Allan has identified five south Devon quarries in use before 1600.[12] Documentary evidence referred to in Chapter 1[13], indicates a thriving coastal trade in the medieval period from the twelfth century and Devon slates were used for roofing superior buildings all along the south coast as far as Essex. The system of laying in diminishing courses was undoubtedly exported, along with the slates. A roofing system which used small slates (those known from archaeological collections range from 4½ ins to 12ins (110-300mm) from peg hole to tail) optimized the use of the output from the quarries and made a serviceable roofing out of pieces that would be rejected within the modern industry of standard sizes.

In Devon we must assume that costs of carriage, whether by sea or overland, restricted the use of slate to those with the deepest pockets. Archaeological evidence of locally sourced slates has been found at Okehampton Castle and on the fourteenth-century guest hall at Buckfast Abbey. Exeter Cathedral owned slate quarries at Penn and Recca, at Staverton, and presumably used this source for the clergy houses and colleges in Cathedral Close. It is likely that close to the quarries, slate may have roofed much more humble buildings than the castles and guest halls of the aristocracy and the Church.

In the seventeenth century the use of slate on the fashionable merchants' houses with timber-framed fronts in Plymouth, Barnstaple and Exeter (see Chapter 6) contributed to a sense of difference between urban building in Devon and the thatched houses of the countryside. Overland carriage must have been far more costly than by water, making the Devon port towns the most likely candidates for early slate roofing, whether or not they were close to quarries.

Surviving pre-nineteenth century Devon roofing slate is extremely rare. Richard Polwhele reckoned that some Devon slate roofs lasted for a century.[14] The crucial factor in lifespan is not always the slate itself, which can often be recycled, but the method of fixing which eventually fails as a result of age and the stresses and strains of weather on the roof. It is some surprise then, that three examples of Devon slate roofs from open hall houses have been preserved, two at Chittlehampton (*pers comm* N.W. Alcock) and one farmhouse at Mariansleigh. The underside of the slates are smoke-blackened from the open hearth fire and each has been thatched over, protecting them from weathering. All three houses are of good, but not gentry, quality They suggest that there may have been rather more slate roofs over the county's rural open halls than had been imagined.

These may later have been stripped off and replaced with thatch, perhaps when a different owner found reslating beyond his means. This is confirmed by fragmentary evidence of former slate roofing found in a handful of superior farmhouses. The houses may have thatched or modern slate roofs today, but loose peggies survive on the wall-tops or may still be attached to an old lath under a later roof.

In the early eighteenth century 'Rag' slates are referred to in Devon documentation but these seems to have been less common than in Cornwall. Today most surviving rag slate roofs are to be found in north-west Devon (8.7). Research by Roger Green has shown that the term appears slightly earlier in Cornish glebe terriers where rags seem initially to have been used on inferior buildings and largely confined to east Cornwall.[15] Rag slates, cut to shape on three sides but with a 'ragged' top edge, vary in size but their dimensions are sometimes given as 2ft x 3ft (600 x 900mm). They are always large enough to be nailed or pegged to the rafters, dispensing with the need for laths. Why they should have been available in quantity in *c.* 1700, but apparently not before, is something of a puzzle. Their arrival may be connected with the use of gunpowder in the slate quarries, allowing larger blocks to be won.

Fires that spread rapidly across the thatched roofs of Devon's smaller towns encouraged the use of slate roofing in the eighteenth century. This practical reason for using slate was supported by changing architectural fashion. The national style of Georgian building promoted sleeker surfaces and was employed in the early nineteenth century expansions of

8.7. *Rag slates on a nineteenth century barn at Dringwell, Thrushelton.*

Exeter, but particularly Plymouth, which was well served by the South Hams slate quarries. John Allan has identified over fifty known slate quarries in South Devon alone,[16] although there has been no comprehensive study of how long each was worked. The photographic record shows that local – either Devon or Cornish – peggies continued to be used to roof terraces of early nineteenth century houses. After 1850 the number of working Devon quarries dwindled to about twenty-five[17] and there were no Devon quarries producing roofing slate after about 1920.

What happened to an industry that had played such an important role in Devon's economy in the medieval period and served its traditional buildings so well, right through to the early nineteenth century? From the late eighteenth century, the Welsh slate industry began to outpace all other British slate sources. Capital investment in Welsh slate quarrying saw the building of railway lines from the mountains, where Welsh slate was produced, down to newly-improved harbours from which it could be exported. The sheer scale of operations in Wales, along with technological advances in cutting slate, altered the whole picture both of roofing slate and of slate hanging. Slates of regular widths and lengths could be produced economically by sorting for size at the quarry, production being assisted by steam-powered saws for cutting.[18] These slates were called 'sized' slates and were given picturesque names: 'ladies', 'duchesses', 'queens', and the like. When laid, the courses did not diminish except at the ridge. Sized slates provided a uniformity and geometry that had never been part of the vernacular tradition. They required less skill to fit than the old system of diminishing courses and, crucial to a building industry coping with expanding housing in urban areas, far less time.

Welsh slate was ordered in bulk by the Navy for its south coast dockyards and seems first to have arrived in Plymouth in about 1830. The system of peggies continued to be used locally for a while, side-by-side with Welsh slate, including on buildings owned by the Navy. Nevertheless, a taste for sized slates had been introduced and the Devon quarries simply could not keep up with it. Cann Quarry was producing 'small ladies' in the 1820s, but this seems to have been the best the Devon quarries could achieve. The quarries were too small

and perhaps the Devon geology unsuitable for the commercial production of sized roofing slates to match those from Wales. The output of the Devon quarries for roofing continued to be peggies and rags. Delabole in Cornwall was the only South West quarry that managed to keep up with the competition by capitalization and combining several independent quarries in 1841 but it never produced the range of sizes that came out of Wales.

The old system of peggies slid down the social scale at speed. It was increasingly likely to be found only on humble buildings, including farm buildings close to the quarries, and less likely to be found on new houses. By 1845 John Hayward, the major church architect in the county, was specifying Welsh duchess slates, to be nailed to red deal laths, and fixed with two wrought copper nails, one in each side, for the church roof at Whimple in east Devon.[19] No lime mortar was mentioned. In 1848, George Wightwick, a Plymouth architect, described the types of slating an architect might specify. He called pegged slates, still using oak lath and oak pins with lime and hair plaster, 'common slating'. These undoubtedly came from South West sources. He described as 'better slating', large or small lady slates 16" x 8" (400 x 200mm) or 14" x 8" (350 x 200mm) nailed into battens, but still plastered beneath. 'Improved slating' included rags, but all the other types were large sized slates: queens, princesses and imperials, and must have come from Wales.[20] By the time of the Great Exhibition at the Crystal Palace in 1851, the Welsh quarries were exhibiting a bewildering range of fancy slates including red duchess slates cut with green diamonds, slates sawn along the bottom edge and slates cut by Matthews patent slate cutting machine. Delabole exhibited rags and a slate cistern, while Devon, the region that had produced slate for royal palaces in the twelfth century, did not have a single exhibit.

Although the Devon slate quarries closed down, the craft of laying peggies and rags was maintained. Survival was motivated by thriftiness in keeping old slate roofs maintained and was refreshed and amended by the Arts & Crafts Movement of the late nineteenth and early twentieth centuries. It continues today, supported by enthusiasm for the vernacular traditions of the county.

Notes and References

Abbreviations

DRO   Devon County Record Office
Med Arch   *Medieval Archaeology*
TDA   *Transactions of the Devonshire Association*
PDAS   *Proceedings of the Devon Archaeological Society*

Introduction

1. Hewison R. *The Heritage Industry* (1987) discusses the wider cultural and political background to these changes from a highly critical stand-point.
2. See valuable series of early articles on church houses by Copeland G.W. *TDA* **92–7** (1960–65).
   Examples of Devon priests' houses are illustrated in Pantin W.A. 'Medieval Priests' Houses in South West England' *Med Arch* **1** (1957) 118–146.
3. Child P. 'Farmhouse Building Traditions' in *Devon's Traditional Buildings* ed. Beacham P. (DCC 1978).
4. Laithwaite M. 'Town Houses up to 1700' in *Devon's Traditional Buildings*.
5. Hoskins W.G. 'Introduction' to *Devon's Traditional Buildings*.

Chapter 1: Local Building Materials and Methods

1. For national surveys of vernacular buildings see Mercer E. *English Vernacular Houses* (1975) Brunskill R.W. *Traditional Buildings of Britain* (1981) and Barley M. *Houses and History* (1986). Other national surveys of particular relevance to south-west England are Smith P. *Houses of the Welsh Countryside* (1988) and Meirion-Jones G.I. *The Vernacular Architecture of Brittany* (1982). The Breton parallels to the longhouse and the upper hall house are especially instructive. See also Fossiea J.C.R. (translated by Cleere H.) *The Village and House in the Middle Ages* (1975).
2. The national context of the Devon cruck tradition is fully described and illustrated in Alcock N.W. *Cruck Construction. An introduction and catalogue* CBA Research Report No. 42 (1981).
3. Harrison J.R. 'The mud wall in England at the Close of the Vernacular Era' *Trans Ancient Mons Soc* Vol 28 (1984) 154–174. This examines the nature of the building materials and puts Devon cob into the national context of mud wall construction: there are extensive references to other sources and parallels. Williams-Ellis C. and Eastwick-Field J. and E. make some references to Devon cob in *Building in Cob, Pisé and Stabilised Earth* (1950) including an account of Ernest Gimson's construction of a cob house (Coxon, near Budleigh Salterton) in 1910. *Mud Hut News* Nos. **1** and **2** (1977 and 1978) describe a modern Devon County Council Architects' Department experiment with unfired earth brick construction. The Devon Historic Buildings Trust has published two excellent pamphlets on 'The Cob Buildings of Devon'; 1 History, Building Methods and Conservation, 1992; and 2 Repair and Maintenance (by Larry Keefe) 1993.
4. Laycock C.H. 'The Old Devon Farm House' *TDA* **52** (1920) 180.
5. For a fuller account see Alec Clifton Taylor's 'Building Stones' in *The Buildings of England: Devon* by Cherry B. and Pevsner N. (1989).
6. There is information on the early slate industry in Devon in Jope E.M. and Dunning E.C., 'The Use of Blue Slates for Roofing in Medieval England' *Antiquaries Journal* Vol xxxiv (1954). By 1187 over 800 000 Devon slates had been brought to Winchester alone for the King's buildings according to Clifton-Taylor in *The Pattern of English Building* (1972) 165. Devon slate in Sussex is discussed with a distribution map of the quarries around Kingsbridge in Houlden E.W. *Slates Roofs in Medieval Sussex* Sussex Archaeological Collections **103** (1965) 67–78. The most recent research is Allan J.P. *Medieval and Post Medieval Finds from Exeter 1971–80* Exeter Archaeological Reports No. 3 (1984) 300–303. This includes a more comprehensive distribution map of slate beds and known quarries in South Devon; the number of slate quarries is remarkable.
7. This slate technique is described and illustrated by Setchell G.T. and

Setchell J. in *The Delabole System of Random Slating in Diminishing Courses.*

8. The technique is discussed and illustrated in *Tuck Pointing in Practice* SPAB Information Leaflet No. 8 (1988).

9. For further information on the brick tile methods see A. Arschavair 'False Fronts in Minor Domestic Architecture' *Trans Ancient Mon. Soc.* **4** (1956) 110–122 and Exwood M. 'Mathematical Tiles' *Vernacular Architecture* Vol 12 (1981) 48–54.

10. The Peters Marland (or simply Marland) brick industry is described in Strong's *Industries of North Devon* (Michael 1899) 163–174. There are numerous illustrations of Marland brick in Michael Laithwaite's 'Victorian Ilfracombe' [Devon Books 1992].

11. Introductory accounts of lime technology are available in the SPAB Information Leaflets No. 1 *Basic Limewash* by Schofield J. and No. 9 *An Introduction to Building Limes* by Wingate M. For more historical and technical details see Ashurst J. *Mortars, Plasters and Renders in Conservation* (Ecclesiastical Architects and Surveyors Association 1984), and Ashurst J. and N. *Mortars, Plaster and Renders* English Heritage Technical Handbook No. 3 (1988). See also 'Appropriate Plasters, Renders and Finishes for Cob and Random Stone Walls in Devon', Devon Earth Building Association 1993 and Jane Schofield 'Lime in Building – A Practical Guide' Black Dog Press 1994.

12. Reprinted in Gilbert C., Lomax J. and Wells-Cole A. *Country House Floors 1660–1850* (Temple Newsam Country House Studies No. 3 1987).

13. The best historically informed approach to the conservation of thatch and the different English traditions is Brockett P. and Wright A. *The Care and Repair of Thatched Roofs* SPAB Technical Pamphlet 10 (1986). *Thatch and Thatching* by Fearn J. (Shire Album 16 1978) also describes the different traditions but the most detailed account, including the different materials and their application to the roof, can be found in *The Thatcher's Craft* (COSIRA 1961).

Chapter 2: Farmhouse Building Traditions

1. Vancouver C. *General View of the Agriculture of the County of Devon*, (1808, reprinted David and Charles 1969)
2. Hoskins W.G. *Devon* (1974)
3. Ibid. 91
4. Fox H. 'Peasant farmers, patterns of settlement and *pays*: transformations in the landscape of Devon and Cornwall in the later Middle Ages' in Higham R. (ed.) *Landscape and Townscape in the South West* (University of Exeter 1989) 41–73.
5. Laithwaite M. 'Middlemoor, Sowton: a re-assessment.' *TDA* **103** (1971) 77–83

6. Alcock N.W. and Laithwaite J.M.W. 1973, 'Medieval houses in Devon and their modernisation.' *Med Arch* **17** (1973) 118–121
7. Ibid. 104–5
8. Hulland C., 'Devonshire Farmhouses V', *TDA* **112** (1980) 159–164
9. Ibid. 128–136
10. Child P.C. and Laithwaite J.M.W. 'Little Rull – a late medieval house near Cullompton', *PDAS* **33** (1975) 303–310
11. Alcock N.W. and Laithwaite J.M.W. op. cit. 112–114
12. Ibid. 114–116
13. Thorp J. 'Wall Painting and Lime Plaster Decoration' This Volume.
14. Williams E.H.D. 'Poltimore Farmhouse, Farway', *TDA* **106** (1974) 215–230
15. Hulland C. op. cit. 142
16. Ibid. 146–153
17. Alcock N.W. 'Houses in an East Devon Parish', *TDA* **94** (1962) 195–201
18. Hulland C. 'Devonshire Farmhouses VI', *TDA* **116** (1984) 29–37
19. Ibid. 48–52
20. Alcock N.W. 'Devonshire Farmhouses I' *TDA* **100** (1968) 14–18
21. Alcock N.W. 'Devonshire Farmhouses IV', *TDA* **104** (1972) 36–40
22. Alcock N.W. 'A Devon Farm – Bury Barton, Lapford', *TDA* **98** (1966) 105–131
23. Machin R. *The Houses of Yetminster* (Bristol University 1978)

Chapter 3: The Longhouse

1. The definition of the longhouse has been, and still is, subject to considerable debate. For the historical background to the use of the term, see Mercer E. 'Domus Longa and Longhouse', *Vernacular Architecture* **III** (1972) 9–10. There is discussion and illustration in all the national vernacular surveys (see bibliography). The Dartmoor National Park Authority has recently commissioned a comprehensive inventory of longhouse literature and records related to Dartmoor from Keystone Historic Building Consultants. This aims to provide a basis for future systematic research which is the essential next step after the valuable but necessarily selective investigations of recent years.

2. See Alcock N.W. 'Devonshire Farmhouses II: Some Dartmoor Houses', *TDA* **101** (1969) for an illustrated account of West Chapple.

3. See Jones S.R. 'Devonshire Farmhouses III: Moorland and non Moorland Longhouses' *TDA* **103** (1971) for an illustrated account of Higher Grenofen, and Pizwell, Lydford.

4. Worth R.H. *Dartmoor* (1953 reprinted David and Charles 1967) contains a pioneering essay on the longhouse with a four-fold typology showing varying degrees of separation between house and

shippon. Note the adapted version of this typology in Barley, M.W.: *The English Farmhouse and Cottage* (1961)

5. See Alcock N.W., Child P.C. and Laithwaite J.M.W. 'Sanders, Lettaford. A Devon Long House' *DAS* **30** (1972) 227–233

6. A comparative analysis of priest and lay houses is made in Pantin W.A. 'Medieval Priests' Houses in South West England' *Med Arch* **1** (1957) 118–146

7. Excavation at Hennard have revealed substantial dual purpose houses incorporating either a storage area or an animal shelter at the lower end from the early or mid nineteenth century as well as an earlier longhouse at Shop.

8. There is a considerable literature on these excavated sites and continuing discussion on their significance in the context of research into medieval settlement patterns in the countryside. See Austin D., 'Dartmoor and the upland village of the south west of England' from Hooke D. (ed.) *Medieval Villages* OUCA Monograph 5 (1985) and 'Excavations in Okehampton Deer Park Devon' (1976–78) *PDAS* **36** (1978) 191–239; Beresford G. 'Three Deserted Medieval Settlements on Dartmoor' *Med Arch* **23** (1979) 98–158; Dyer C. 'English Peasant Buildings in the Late Middle Ages' *Med Arch* **30** (1986) 19–45: Jope E.M. and Thelfall R.I. 'Excavations of a Medieval Settlement at Beere North Tawton, Devon' *Med Arch* **2** (1958) 112–40

9. Mercer E. *English Vernacular Houses* (HMSO 1975) pp. 34–49

10. Swete J. *Picturesque Sketches of Devon 1792–1801*, reprinted in *Devon's Age of Elegance*, ed. Hunt P. (Devon Books 1984) 88–90

Chapter 4: Farm Buildings

1. White W. *History, Gazeteer and Directory of Devonshire* (1850, reprinted David and Charles 1968) 35–6

2. Vancouver C. *General View of the Agriculture of the County of Devonshire* (1808 reprinted David and Charles 1969) 209

3. Marshall W. *Rural Economy of the West of England*, Vol 1 (1796, reprinted David and Charles 1970) 184–5

4. Alcock N.W. 'The Medieval Buildings of Bishops Clyst' *TDA* **98** (1966) 133–8

5. I am indebted to Roger Robinson for showing and explaining these barns to me.

6. Seale Hayne Agricultural College *Some Notes on Agriculture in Devon* (1935)

7. Marshall op. cit. 61–2

8. Hoskins W.G. *History From The Farm* (Faber 1970) 46

9. Marshall op. cit. 114

10. Marshall op. cit. 256–7
11. Marshall op. cit. 274
12. Hoskins W.G. *Devon* (David and Charles 1974) 152
13. Worth R.H. *Worth's Dartmoor* (David and Charles 1967)
14. Information from Mr T. Authers of Burrow Farm, Holcombe Rogus
15. Ellacott S.E. *Braunton Farms and Farmers* (Aycliffe Press 1981)
16. Vancouver C. op. cit. 472–4

Chapter 5: Town Houses up to 1660

1. *Gentleman's Magazine*, May 1799 369

2. 44 High Street also had an external side-passage originally, blocked by building a house over it in the seventeenth century.

3. The Three Tuns appears to have been converted, by the seventeenth century, into a house with one deep room on the first floor, heated by two fireplaces.

4. Examples are also known in Bristol, Chester, London, Taunton and York, although in some cases either the gallery or the back block has been demolished.

5. Probate Inventory of John West of Tiverton, 1630: DRO, unsorted.

6. DRO 2065/add 3

Chapter 6: Town Houses of the late Seventeenth and early Eighteenth Centuries

1. Hoskins W.G. *Industry, Trade and People in Exeter 1688–1800* (University of Exeter 2nd edition 1968)

2. Stephens W.B. 'Merchant Companies and Commercial Policy in Exeter 1625–88' *TDA* **86** (1954) 155

3. Allan J.P. *The Medieval and Post-medieval Finds from Exeter 1971–80*. Exeter Archaeological Reports 3 (1984) fig. 135

4. Portman D. *Exeter Houses, 1400–1700* (Exeter University 1966) 59

5. Laithwaite M. 'Totnes Houses 1500–1800' from *The Transformation of English Provincial Towns, 1600–1800* ed. Clark P. (Hutchinson 1985)

6. Kelsall F. 'The London house plan in the later 17th century' *Post Medieval Archaeology* **8** (1974) 80–9

7. *Bideford Bridge Trust Account Book* DRO Ref. B6/1

8. Defoe D. *A Tour Through England and Wales Vol 1* ed. Rhys E. (1928) 260

9. Laithwaite op. cit. 89

Chapter 7: Wall Painting and Lime Plaster Decoration

1. French K. and C. 'Devonshire Plasterwork' *TDA* **89** (1957) 124–144
2. Wilson R.E. 'Tudor and Merton Cottages, Sidmouth' *TDA* **106** (1974) 155–9
3. Beard G. *Decorative Plasterwork in Great Britain* (Phaidon 1975)
4. Fouracre J.T. 'Ornamental lime-plaster ceilings and the plasterer's craft in Devonshire'. *TDA* **41** (1909) 256–262
5. Beard op. cit. 29
6. Oliver B. 'The early seventeenth-century plaster ceilings of Barnstaple'. *TDA* **49** (1917) 190–199
7. Brook I. 'The Riddle of Devon plasterers'. *Country Life* 29 December 1950 2214–16
8. French C. Illustrated correspondence in *Country Life* 18 April 1957 774
9. French K. and C. op. cit. 128
10. French K. and C. op. cit. 136–40
11. French K. and C. op. cit. 126
12. Beard op. cit. 33–52
13. Portman D. *Exeter Houses, 1400–1700* (1966) 42n
14. Lega-Weekes E. report in West Country Studies Library, Exeter
15. It is preserved in the Bideford Community Archive
16. French K. and C. op. cit. 133
17. Beard op. cit. 52

Chapter 8: Recent Research Projects in Devon

1. English Heritage. *Dendrochronology. Guidelines on producing and interpreting dendrochronological dates* (1998) 4
2. English Heritage *op cit* 5
3. Cathy Groves of the University of Sheffield Dendrochronology Laboratory has compiled a summary of the success rates for medieval and post-medieval standing buildings (dated samples as a percentage of processed samples). The national figure is calculated from the tree-ring lists published in *Vernacular Architecture* (volumes 20–28, 1989–1997). The Devon figures are calculated from information available in *Vernacular Architecture* (volumes 11–29, 1980–1998) and that provided by various of her colleagues.
4. Hulland C. 'Devonshire Farmhouses V', TDA **112** (1980) 128–36
5. English Heritage is publishing a monograph on the history and archaeology of Bowhill, written by Stuart Blaylock, in 2002.
6. John Letts' work *Smoke Blackened Thatch* was published jointly by English Heritage and the University of Reading in 1999. This was followed by two volumes, 5 and 6, in the English Heritage Research Transactions series: *Thatch: Thatching in England 1700–1940* by James Moir and John Letts and *Thatch: Thatching in England 1940–1994* by Jo Cox and John Letts.
7. 'Medieval Houses in Devon and their Modernization' in *Medieval Archaeology* **17** (1973) 100–125.
8. This account of the slate roofing tradition in Devon is heavily indebted to several general books and articles. Publications additional to those cited in notes below are:
   Bennett F. & Pinion A. *Roof Slating and Tiling* (1935).
   Born A. 'Blue Slate Quarrying in South Devon', *Industrial Archaeology Review*, 11 No 1 (Autumn 1988), 51–67.
   Jope E.M. & Dunning G.C. 'The use of blue slate for roofing in medieval England', *The Antiquaries Journal*, 34 (1954) 208–217.
   Portman D. *Exeter Houses 1400–1700* (Exeter, The University, 1966).
9. Oliver Bosence, *pers.comm.*
10. Cox J. & Thorp J.R.L., 'Authentic Slating in Devon', *Association for Studies in the Conservation of Historic Buildings Transactions* 16 (1992) 3–12, 6.
11. Morris C. (ed.) *The Journeys of Celia Fiennes*, (1947), 251.
12. Allan J.P. *Medieval and Post-Medieval Finds from Exeter 1971–1980*, Exeter Archaeological Reports 3 (1984), 301.
13. Chapter 1, p.23 and note 6.
14. Polwhele R. *The History of Devonshire* (1793–1806), 52.
15. Green Roger C. 'Common Rags and Scantles: Traditional Methods of Slate Roofing in Cornwall'. Thesis for PgDip Architecture Conservation Course at the School of Architecture, University of Plymouth, June 1995.
16. Allan, *op cit.*
17. Bowman A.C. 'A Historical Survey of Quarry Companies and Operators in Devon and Cornwall'. Author's typescript combining information from the published mineral statistics and unofficial sources.
18. Correspondence with Dr Michael Lewis, Department of History, University of Hull, stimulated by a 1995 Public Inquiry into the source and type of historic slates used on the buildings of the Royal William Yard, Stonehouse, Plymouth.
19. Devon RO, 1418 A add 2/PW 1.
20. Wightwick G. *Hints to Young Architects* (1847) 106.

Illustration credits

Photographs and drawings are reproduced by kind permission of the following:

The Association for Studies in the Conservation of Historic Buildings (John Thorp): 8.5; Peter Beacham: 1.6, 1.8, 1.12, 1.13, 1.14, 1.15, 3.2, 3.3, 3.6, 3.12 (top), 3.13, plates 1–4, 8, 9; Brian Blakeway: 1.1, 1.2, 2.2, 2.3 (right), 2.6, 3.1, 4.2, 4.6, 4.7, 4.10; Jane Brayne: 6.8; Chris Chapman: 3.5 (top), 3.7, plate 11; Peter Child: 2.5, 2.8, 2.9, 2.10, 2.11, 2.12, 2.13, 2.14, 4.11, 4.12, 4.16, 8.7, plates 5, 7, 10; Council for British Archaeology: 1.3; Country Life: 7.25; Jo Cox (Keystone): 8.6; Devon and Exeter Institution: plate 14; Devon County Council: 1.11, 2.3 (left), 2.4, 2.7, 5.8, 5.11, 5.12, 5.15, 7.3, 7.20; Devon County Record Office: 5.6, plate 13; Exeter Museums Archaeological Field Unit: 3.4, 3.6, 3.8, 3.9, 3.11, 5.10, 7.2, 7.37; Frances Griffith: 4.17, 4.18, plate 6; George H. Hall: 7.5; Michael Laithwaite: 5.14; Ralph Mackridge: 3.10, 5.1, 5.2, 5.3, 5.4, 5.5, 5.7, 5.17, 5.18, 6.2, 6.4 (top), plate 12; National Monuments Record: 5.13; Penguin Books Ltd (*The Buildings of England: Devon*): 1.5, 6.7, 6.10; Kate Procter (Dartmoor National Park Authority): 3.4, 3.12 (bottom); James Ravilious: pages 8, 10, 12; 1.7, 1.9, 1.10, 1.16, 1.17, 2.1, 4.1, 4.3, 4.5, 4.8, 4.9, 4.13, 4.19; Roger Robinson: 4.4; Royal Albert Memorial Museum, Exeter: 7.27, 7.28; John Thorp (Keystone): 6.1, 6.2, 6.3, 6.4 (bottom), 6.5, 6.6, 6.9, 6.11, 6.12, 6.13, 6.14, 6.15, 7.1, 7.12, 7.13, 7.14, 7.15, 7.16, 7.17, 7.18, 7.19, 7.20, 7.21, 7.22, 7.23, 7.24, 7.26, 7.29, 7.30, 7.31, 7.32, 7.33, 7.34, 7.35, 7.36, 7.38, 7.39, 7.40, 7.41, 8.3, plates 15–29; John Thorp and Rupert Ford (Keystone): 8.1, 8.2, 8.4; University of Exeter Press: 5.16.

ACKNOWLEDGEMENT

Cathy Groves of the University of Sheffield Dendrochronology Laboratory commented on the draft of Chapter 8 and provided some of her own unpublished research information.

Bibliography

Abbreviations: see p.150

General

The following national studies provide a general context and contain useful Devon references and examples.

Alcock, N.W. *Cruck Construction: An Introduction and Catalogue* (CBA Research Paper No. 42 1981)

Ayres J. *The Home in Britain: Decoration, Design and Construction of Vernacular Interiors 1500–1850* (Faber 1981)

Brigden R. *Victorian Farms* (Crowood Press 1986)

Barley M.W. 'A Glossary of Names for Rooms in Houses of the Sixteenth and Seventeenth Centuries', in *Culture and Environment*, ed. Foster I. and Alcock L. (Routledge and Kegan Paul 1963)

Barley M.W. *The English Farmhouse and Cottage* (Routledge and Kegan Paul 1961) A pioneering study which must now be related to later research

Barley M.W. *Houses and History* (Faber 1986) Particularly valuable because it places local building traditions in the context of the development of greater houses

Barley M.W. (ed.) *The Buildings of the Countryside* (CUP 1990)

Brunskill R.W. *Illustrated Handbook of Vernacular Architecture* (Faber 3rd Edition 1987) The classic guide, first published in 1971, to the systematic study of building construction, plan-form and architectural detail

Brunskill R.W. *Traditional Buildings of Britain* (Gollanz 1981)

Brunskill R.W. *Traditional Farm Buildings of Britain* (2nd ed. Gollanz 1987)

Clifton-Taylor A. *The Pattern of English Building* (Faber 4th ed. 1987) Indispensable for building materials and methods

Darley G. *The National Trust Book of the Farm* (National Trust 1981)

Harris R. *Discovering Timber Framed Buildings* (Shire 1978) The best brief introduction to a complex subject

Harvey N. *A History of Farm Buildings in England and Wales* (David and Charles 2nd Edition 1984)

Innocent C.F. *The Development of English Building Construction* (Cambridge University Press 1916, reprinted David and Charles 1971) Rather northern in emphasis but with much rare information

McCann J. *Clay and Cob Buildings* (Shire 1983)

Mercer E. *English Vernacular Houses* (HMSO 1975)

Peters J.E.C. *Discovering Traditional Farm Buildings* (Shire 1981)

Smith P. *Houses of the Welsh Countryside* (HMSO 2nd ed. 1988)

Taylor C. *Village and Farmstead: A History of Rural Settlement in England* (George Philip 1983) Provides a historical context for local rural building

Thirsk J. (ed) *The Agrarian History of England and Wales*, Vol IV 1500–1640, Vol V 1640–1750 (Cambridge University Press 1967, 1985)

William E. *The Historical Farm Buildings of Wales* (John Donald 1986)

Regional Studies

This brief selection gives examples of other regional surveys which are relevant to Devon because of their comparative value in treating similar historic contexts and building types, or their geographical proximity.

Carter A. and Wade Martins S. (eds) *A Year in the Field* The Norfolk Historic Farm Buildings Project, Centre for East Anglian Studies (University of East Anglia 1987)

Chesher V.M. and F.J. *The Cornishman's House* (Bradford Barton 1968) A pioneering county study.

Fox C. and Lord Raglan *Monmouthshire Houses* Vols I–III (National Museum of Wales 1951–4) The classic study which substantially influenced Hoskins 'Great Rebuilding' thesis.

Fox H. 'Peasant farmers, patterns of settlement and *pays:* transformations in the landscape of Devon and Cornwall in the later Middle Ages', in Higham R. (ed.) *Landscape and Townscape in the South West* (University of Exeter 1989)

Harrison B. and Hutton B. *Vernacular Houses in North Yorkshire and Cleveland* (John Donald 1984) Valuable for its placing of vernacular housing in its social and economic context.

Machin R. *The Houses of Yetminster* (University of Bristol 1978) Exemplary demonstration of the importance of documentary research in providing the social and economic history of local building.

Meirion-Jones G.I. *The Vernacular Architecture of Brittany* (John Donald 1982) Interesting parallels with south-west England.

RCHM (England) *Houses of the North York Moors* (HMSO 1987)

RCAHM (Wales) *Inventory of Ancient Monuments in Glamorgan* IV Part II Farmhouses and Cottages (HMSO 1988) The most substantial recent survey to combine agrarian and building history.

Devon

W.G. Hoskins provides much social and economic background: his *Devon* (1954, reprinted David and Charles 1974), is indispensable. Several agrarian and building history essays by him and H.P.R. Finberg were published as *Devonshire Studies* in 1952 reprinted as *Old Devon* and *West Country Historical Studies* by their respective authors in 1966.

The revised *Devon* volume in the *Buildings of England* series (Penguin 1989) by Bridget Cherry and Nikolaus Pevsner is also essential reading as a comprehensive account of the architectural history of the county.

Rural Building

Many systematic studies of rural building in Devon have been published in recent years as the list below indicates, their chronology reflecting the developing understanding of the subject. For information about a particular building the reader is encouraged to use the revised statutory lists of buildings of architectural and historic interest for rural Devon. (Copies are available for public inspection at County Hall and the relevant District Council Offices.) Many of the lists provide far more than a basic description of the building, often including an analysis of the building's development and sometimes even documentary references.

Alcock N.W. 'Houses in an East Devon Parish' *TDA* **94** (1962) 185–232 The first systematic survey of local building in a Devon parish

Alcock N.W. 'Devonshire Linhays – A Vernacular Tradition' *TDA* **95** (1963) 117–130

Alcock N.W. 'The Medieval Houses of Bishops Clyst' *Med Arch* (1965) 146–153

Alcock N.W. 'The Medieval Buildings of Bishops Clyst' *TDA* **98** (1966) 133–153

Alcock N.W. 'A Devon Farm – Bury Barton, Lapford' *TDA* **98** (1966) 105–131

Alcock N.W. 'Devon Farmhouses I' *TDA* **100** (1968) 13–28

Alcock N.W. 'Devon Farmhouses II' *TDA* **101** (1969) 83–106

Alcock N.W. and Hulland C. 'Devon Farmhouses IV' *TDA* **104** (1972) 35–57

Alcock N.W., Child P.C. and Laithwaite J.M.W. 'Sanders, Lettaford – A Devon Longhouse' *PDAS* **30** (1972) 227–233

Alcock N.W. and Laithwaite J.M.W. 'Medieval Houses in Devon and their modernisation' *Med Arch* **17** (1973) 100–126 The most important essay for understanding the evolution of the late medieval house through into the later sixteenth and seventeenth centuries.

Alcock N.W. (ed) *Dartington Houses – A Survey* (Exeter Papers in Industrial Archaeology No. 3 University of Exeter 1972)

Beacham P.M. 'Rural Building 1400–1800' in Cherry B. and Pevsner N. *The Buildings of England: Devon* (Penguin 1989)

Beacham P.M. 'The Dartmoor Longhouse' *Devon Archaeology* **3** (1985)

Beacham P.M. (ed) *Devon's Traditional Buildings* (Devon County Council 1978)

Beacham P.M. 'Local Building, Traditions in Devon from the Medieval Period to 1700' in *Archaeology of the Devon Landscape* ed. Timms S. (Devon County Council 1980)

Brown S.W. and Pidgeon J. 'Hatherleigh Farm, Bovey Tracey' *PDAS* **44** (1986) 184–191

Cash M.E. (ed) *Devon Inventories of the 16th and 17th Centuries* (Devon and Cornwall Record Society New Series 11 1966)

Child P.C. and Laithwaite J.M.W. 'Little Rull – A Late Medieval House near Cullompton' *PDAS* **33** (1975) 303–310

Copeland G.W. 'Devonshire Church Houses' *TDA* **92–7** (1960–65) A series of six articles forming a cumulative inventory with many photographs.

Egeland P. *Cob and Thatch* (Devon Books 1988)

Harrison J.R. 'The Mud Wall in England at the Close of the Vernacular Era' *Trans Ancient Monuments Society* **28** (1984) 154–174 Indispensable account of both the basic technology and Devon specialities.

Havinden M. and Wilkinson F. 'Farming' in *Dartmoor – A New Study* ed. Crispin Gill (David and Charles 1970) Useful information on agrarian history of the moor.

Jones S.R. 'Devon Farmhouses III: Moorland and Non Moorland Longhouses' *TDA* **103** (1971) 35–76

Lomas J. 'Higher Hareston, Brixton' *TDA* **106** (1974) 119–140

Marshall W. *Rural Economy of the West of England* (1796, reprinted David and Charles 1970)

Morley B. 'Leigh Barton, Churchstow' *PDAS* **41** (1983) 81–106

Pantin W.A. 'Medieval Priest's Houses in South West England' *Med Arch* **1** (1957) 118–146

Williams E.H.D. 'Poltimore Farmhouse, Farway' *TDA* **106** (1974) 215–230

Williams E.H.D. 'Curing Chambers and Domestic Corn Drying Kilns' *Somerset Archeological and Natural History Society* **120** (1976) 57–61 Includes Devon examples.

Wilson R. 'Tudor and Merton Cottages, Sidmouth' *TDA* **106** (1974)

155–160
Worth R.H. 'The Dartmoor House' in *Dartmoor* (David and Charles 1967) 405–418 Includes Worth's pioneering typology of the longhouse.
Vancouver C. *General View of the Agriculture of the County of Devon* (1808, reprinted by David and Charles 1969)

Urban buildings

Much research has now been published on this subject, although the amount awaiting publication is still considerable. The latter includes surveys by the Exeter Museums Archaeological Field Unit, S.R. Jones (Plymouth), J.M.W. Laithwaite (Totnes and elsewhere) and the North Devon District Council Rescue Archaeological Unit (Barnstaple). The revised statutory lists for the town centres of Bideford and Ilfracombe, compiled by Michael Laithwaite, have been published and revised lists for Barnstaple and Tiverton are due out soon.

Barber James 'No. 4 Vauxhall Street, Plymouth' *TDA* **105** (1973) 17–35
'No. 33 St Andrew's Street, Plymouth' *TDA* **105** (1973) 37–54
Barber Jennifer 'Yogge's House or Prysten House?' *TDA* **105** (1973) 75–86
Blaylock S.R. 'An Architectural Survey of the Late Medieval Hall at Plymouth Gin Distillery' *PDAS* **43** (1985) 121–125 The Black Friars building.
Chapman S.D. (ed) *The Devon Cloth Industry in the Eighteenth Century: Sun Fire Office Inventories of Merchants' and Manufacturers' Property 1726–1770* (Devon and Cornwall Record Society New Series 23 1978) Useful for building materials and outbuildings in towns.
Davison A. and Henderson C.G. 'Archaeological Investigations at Fore Street, Totnes *Exeter Archaeology 1984–5* (Exeter Museums Archaeological Field Unit 1985) Discusses Little Priory: historical notes by J.M.W. Laithwaite.
Dunkley J.A. Henderson C.G. and Allan J.P. 'Survey of 5 West Street and 15 Stepcote Hill' *Exeter Archaeology 1984–5* (Exeter Museums Archaeological Field Unit 1985) 36–38
Erskine A.M. and Portman D. 'The History of an Exeter Tenement: 229 High Street' *TDA* **92** (1960) 142–157
Faulkner P.A. 'Medieval Undercrofts and Town Houses' *Archaeological Journal* **123** (1966) 120–135 Discusses 36 North Street, Exeter, in relation to a house in Southampton.
Laithwaite J.M.W. 'Two Medieval Houses in Ashburton' *PDAS* **29** (1971) 181–194
Laithwaite J.M.W. 'Totnes Houses 1500–1800' in *The Transformation of English Provincial Towns* ed. Clark P. (Hutchinson 1985), 62–98

Manpower Services Commission Barnstaple Historic Buildings Survey Vol I, 1985–6 (North Devon District Council)
Nartowski N. *The Prudential Site, 65–68 High Street, Barnstaple* (North Devon District Council Rescue Archaeology Unit, c. 1986)
Oliver B.W. 'The Early Seventeenth-Century Plaster Ceilings of Barnstaple' *TDA* **49** (1917) 190–199
Oliver B.W. 'The Three Tuns Barnstaple' *TDA* **80** (1948) 147–158
O'Neil BH St J and Russell P. '5 Higher Street, Dartmouth' *TDA* **83** (1951) 267–271
Pantin W.A. 'Medieval English Town House Plans' *Med Arch* **6–7** (1962–63) 202–239
Pantin W.A. 'Some Medieval English Town Houses' in *Culture and Environment*, ed. I.L. Foster and L. Alcock (Routledge and Kegan Paul 1963) 445–478
Portman D. *Exeter Houses: 1400–1700* (Exeter University 1966)
Russell P. and Everett A.W. 'The Old House known as Number Thirteen, Higher Street, Dartmouth' *TDA* **91** (1959) 107–111
Thorp J.R.L. 'Two Hall Houses from a late Medieval Terrace, 8–12 Fore Street, Silverton' *PDAS* **40** (1982) 171–180
Thorp J.R.L. '4 The Quay, Dartmouth: a Devon Town-House of 1664' *PDAS* **41** (1983) 107–122
Thorp J.R.L. 'Bridgeland Street, Bideford' in *Devon Buildings Group Newsletter* 4 October 1987 22–26
Topsham Society *Topsham, an account of its streets and buildings* (Topsham Society 1971) A series of historical notes and descriptions, with strip-elevations and a plan of 34 The Strand.
Weddell P.J. 'The Excavation of Medieval and Later Houses at Wolborough Street, Newton Abbot' *PDAS* **43** (1985) 77–109 Includes notes and drawings of former standing buildings.

Building Conservation

Good introductions to the subject are:

Cunnington P. *Care for Old Houses* (Prism Alpha 1984)
Lander H. *The House Restorer's Guide* (David and Charles 1988)
Powys A.R. *The Repair of Ancient Buildings* (Dent 1929 Reprinted SPAB 1984)
Saunders M. *The Historic Home Owner's Companion* (Batsford 1987)

For more technical information see:

SPAB (various authors) Technical Pamphlets and Information Sheets
Ashurst J. and N. *English Heritage Technical Handbooks* Vols 1–5 (HMSO 1988)

Bibliography for third edition

The 1995 second edition of Devon Building incorporated a small selection of new and significant publications into the original bibliography of 1990. This was not a comprehensive list of new works since 1990 and set out below is a list of other works relevant to Devon's traditional architecture published since 1990 and which are not already cited in the 'notes and references' or in the principal bibliography.

Besides the specific references below, other useful material on the subject can be found in the newsletters of the Devon Buildings Group (1986–), copies of which are deposited in the West Country Studies Library in Exeter, reports on buildings produced by Exeter Archaeology (many of which are also in the same library), and reports of the recorders of buildings in the Transactions of the Devonshire Association **128** (1996), **130** (1998) and **131** (1999).

Listed Building entries for all of England are currently available on the Images of England web site: www.imagesofengland.org.uk

Barnwell P.S. and Giles C. *English Farmsteads, 1750–1914* (RCHME 1997). Unfortunately this work does not include Devon in its studies (east Cornwall is as near as it gets) but it is essential reading for those interested in farm buildings and their study.

Blaylock S.R. 'Exeter Guildhall' PDAS **48** (1990) 123–178. A detailed study of one of Exeter's most historic buildings.

Brown S. and Laithwaite M. 'Northwood Farm, Christow; an abandoned Farmstead on the Eastern Fringe of Dartmoor' PDAS **51** (1993) 161–184. A rare instance of the archaeological excavation of a rural farmhouse in Devon.

Brown S. 'Leigh Barton, Churchstow, Devon' PDAS **56** (1998) 5–108. A very detailed analysis of an important fifteenth–seventeenth century rural house.

Cherry B. 'The Devon Country House in the Late Seventeenth and early Eighteenth Centuries' PDAS **46** (1988) 91–135. A seminal account of the larger house in Devon in this period.

Gawne E. and Sanders J. *Early Devon Longhouses: Longhouses in Widecombe* (Orchard Publications 1998) A description and analysis of surviving longhouses in a Dartmoor parish.

Gawne H.E. 'Sweaton Farmhouse' TDA **124** (1992) 167–173

Harrison R. *Earth: the Conservation and Repair of Bowhill, Exeter: Working with Cob* English Heritage Research Transactions Vol 3 (1999). A detailed analysis of the use of cob and its repair in a fifteenth century building.

Henderson C.G. and Weddell P.J. 'Medieval Settlers on Dartmoor and in West Devon: the Evidence from Excavation' *PDAS* **52** (1994) 119–140 A reassessment of previous archaeological work partly in the context of re-excavation. See also note 8 to chapter 3.

Keefe L. and Child P. 'Devon and Cornwall' in *'Terra Britannica'* eds Hurd J. and Gourley B. (ICOMOS UK 2000) 34–39. A short account of earth building in the region in a book which describes the earth tradition in the British Isles.

Laithwaite J.M.W. '1523–1642: Merchants, Money and Markets' in *The Heart of Totnes* eds Bridge M. and Pegg J. 1998

Miles D. 'The Interpretation, Presentation and Use of Tree-Ring Dates' Vernacular Architecture **28** (1997) 40–56. A clear exposition of the scientific methodology of dendrochronology.

Miles T.J. 'The Seventeenth-Century Sgraffito-Decorated Fireplaces at Middle Moor, Sowton' PDAS **47** (1989) 136–8

Musson M. *Topsham Houses, Warehouses and Trades:1700s and earlier.* (Published by the author 1998)

Newton P.H. 'Blagdon Cider Barn, Paignton' TDA **123** (1991) 203–211

Penoyre J. 'Medieval Somerset Roofs' Vernacular Architecture **29** (1998) 22–23. Somerset roofs closely relate to Devon roofs and this study is based on a dendrochronological dating survey of them.

Powell C. 'Cobing and Helling: a Georgian building firm at work' Construction History **15** (1999) 3–13. Describes the work of a Crediton firm which routinely carried out construction in cob.

Richardson I. 'Farm Buildings on the Killerton Estate' Devon Buildings Group Research Papers **1** (1993) 13–31

Thorp J.R.L. 'Carpentry and framing techniques in Devon vernacular building down to 1550' in *Regional Variations in Timber-Famed Building in England and Wales down to 1550* (Essex County Council 1999) A description of all aspects of the use of timber, including roof structures, in Devon vernacular buildings.

Thorp J.R.L. and Cox J. 'The Traditional Dartmoor Farmstead; the End' PDAS **52** (1994) 241–269. Includes a detailed study of one farmstead.

Weddell P.J. and Reed S.J. 'Excavations at Sourton Down, Okehampton 1986-1991; Roman Road, Deserted Medieval Hamlet and Other Features. PDAS **55** (1997) 39–147. Includes excavated thirteenth–fifteenth century longhouses.

Wyatt P (ed) *The Uffculme Wills and Inventories. 16–18th centuries* Devon and Cornwall Record Society New Series Vol 40 1997. This work is a compilation of the probate inventories (which listed the contents of houses on an owner's death) for a Devon parish within the Diocese of Salisbury. Few of these inventories survive for Devon as those for the Diocese of Exeter were destroyed in The Blitz. A separate work interprets the inventories: eds Wyatt P. and Stanes R. *Uffculme: a Peculiar Parish* (Uffculme Archive Group 1997)

Notes on the contributors

Peter Beacham came to Devon in 1967 as the County Council's first historic buildings officer. Working at first with W.G. Hoskins and other colleagues who are fellow contributors to this book, he took a special interest in the farmstead building traditions of the county, resulting in a major essay on rural building history in the second edition of *Devon* in Pevsner's *Buildings of England* series. He joined English Heritage in 1991 and is presently Head of Urban Strategies and Listing. In 2000 he published *Down the Deep Lanes*, a tribute to rural Devon, with his friend the photographer James Ravilious.

Peter Child read archaeology at Cambridge and after post graduate archaeological research there joined the staff of Northampton Museum. Soon after his appointment as an archaeologist with Devon County Council in 1968 he became involved with historic building casework and undertook some of the earliest research into Devon's rural building history with Nat Alcock and Michael Laithwaite. Their joint publication of these systematic early studies proved influential in later research. During 1972–4 he studied at the University of York to obtain a Diploma in Conservation Studies. After gaining wider experience as a planning officer with East Devon District Council he was reappointed to the County Council's environment team in 1985 and is now the County Historic Building Adviser.

Michael Laithwaite worked for the London County Council's Survey of London after reading history at Oxford. In 1966 he became senior research fellow in the department of English Local History at the University of Leicester under Professor W.G. Hoskins. Here he developed his research interest in English towns, concentrating on Burford (Oxfordshire) and Totnes, subsequently publishing important studies of the building history in both towns. After moving to Devon he undertook some of the earliest systematic studies of rural building in the county which resulted in influential publications. He was a member of the Architecton historic building resurvey team before joining the County Council's historic building team from 1986 to 1991. In 1994 he was elected President of the Devon Archaeological Society.

John Thorp developed his interest in Devon building history while reading archaeology at Exeter University. He joined the Exeter Museum's Archaeological Field Unit to undertake major building recording programmes in Exeter and elsewhere in the county. He has published important studies of both urban and rural building history in Devon which made him an invaluable member of the Architecton historic building survey team, on which he served for the whole five year survey period. After the completion of the survey he joined with another member of the Architecton team, Jo Cox, to form a historic buildings consultancy, Keystone, which has subsequently carried out projects throughout England. He and Jo are co-authors of Chapter 8.

Index